Japanese Gardening Hints

JAPANESE GARDENING HINTS

by Katsuo Saito

The romance of gleaming sand,
rugged stones, and shady trees
in your own garden

JAPAN PUBLICATIONS, INC.

Published by Japan Publications, Inc., Tokyo, Japan

Distributed by Japan Publications Trading Company
1255 Howard St., San Francisco, Calif. 94103 U.S.A.
175 Fifth Ave., New York, N.Y. 10010 U.S.A.
P.O. Box 5030 Tokyo International, Tokyo, Japan

Library of Congress Catalog Card No. 68–58251

First printing: August, 1969

Printed in Japan

Preface

I dare say that in the world of publications few people can equal my record for writing prefaces. This is the sixteenth time in a period of forty-eight years that I have composed opening remarks for a work by Katsuo Saito.

On page seventy-five of a book entitled *Teien Kansho-ho* (Ways to Appreciate Gardens), my second work, written when I was still a student, I find the following comment.

"Although we are told that the antithesis between landscape gardens and architecturally oriented gardens is irresolvable, I am so far from believing the two as opposed as fire and water that I feel a solution will certainly be reached in the near future. Furthermore, I believe that the modern garden formalists will be the ones who unravel this thousand-years-old puzzle."

Saito says this passage inspired him to pioneer in the art of gardening, and in that sense I consider him the heir to my philosophy of gardens. The fact that he began his studies of Japanese gardens at the age of sixteen gives a distinctive coloration to his work, which he continues today, both in design and in writing. This characteristic and his wide experience in gardening in other countries lead me to expect something fresh and unusual from his collection of hints. With this expectation in mind, I take the opportunity to express my congratulations to and great faith in a fine artist.

January, 1969   TSUYOSHI TAMURA

Author's Foreword

Japan's oldest written historical account, the *Kojiki* (Record of Ancient Matters) contains a poem describing a brave man who, for the sake of a long life with his beloved wife, built a fence and planted a garden around their house. As human society progressed from this fundamental level, the garden too expanded its significance to include social ties of friendship. For instance, the conventional use of stones and other garden elements for the master of the house and others for the guests represents feelings of mutual trust and understanding and, on the aesthetic level, provides vital balance to traditional landscape designs. A still more intense expression of social ties of trust and friendship is to be found in the serene tea garden, the *roji*.

Although the Japanese garden is often mistakenly believed to consist largely in stately, elaborate landscapes for the mansions of the wealthy or for temples or public buildings, its true nature, as I hope I have shown, is deeply related to fundamental human ties of marital affection and of friendship. In this book, I stress this aspect of Japanese gardens and treat the important design elements of mystery and refined elegance in terms that, I hope, will be meaningful to people in other lands who want either to design Japanese gardens or to incorporate some elements of them in their present garden plans.

I am very grateful to my respected teacher, Tsuyoshi Tamura, for his preface, the sixteenth he has written for me, to Yukishige Takahashi for his diligent editorial work, to Ihei Misaki for his beautiful photographs, and to Richard L. Gage, who translated the manuscript.

March, 1969   KATSUO SAITO

Contents

Preface 5
Author's Foreword 7

I. Characteristics of the Japanese Garden *13*

1. **Subdued, Subtle, and Elegant** *13*
2. **Symbolization** *14*
3. **The Somber Refinement of the Tea Garden** *18*
4. **The Elegance of the Alleyway Garden** *28*
5. **The Subtlety of a Garden with Pond or Fountain** *29*
6. **The Symbolism of the Sand and Rock Garden** *31*

II. Japanese Garden Elements in Various Settings *33*

1. **Apportioning Space** *33*
2. **Gardens with Spacious Lawns** *34*
    A Lawn Garden Overlooking the Sea *34*
    Lawn Visible through a Stand of Black Pines *36*
    A Lawn Garden at the Base of a Cliff *42*
    A Quiet Lawn Garden *45*
    A Garden Symbolizing Natural Fields *47*
    An Open Lawn Garden *49*
    Lawn That Is Also A Golf Training Course *49*
    A Golf Green in a Garden *51*
    A Garden with Shrubbery Pruned in Mountain Shapes *52*
3. **Gardens in Groves** *53*
    A Garden in a Stand of Cryptomeria Cedars *53*
    Miscellaneous Trees with Black Pine *56*
    A Garden in a Black-pine Grove *59*
    Garden in a Grove of Miscellaneous Trees *60*
4. **Gardens with Large Ponds** *61*
    A Bright Pond *61*
    An Elegant Pond *66*
5. **Gardens Combining Stone Groups and Gravel with Moss or Lawn** *67*

9

A Stone Group with Half-concealed Mountains in the Background *67*
A Garden Called the Joys of Entering Nirvana *69*
Using Sand to Symbolize a Calm Body of Water *71*
6. **Gardens for Limited Spaces** *74*
A Garden with Rugged Stones *74*
A Garden in the Shape of a Stream *80*
7. **Front Gardens** *82*
A Large Stone Group of Competing Forces *82*
Front Garden with Parking Space *83*
Front Entrance with a Natural-style Retaining Wall *84*
Birches and a Stone against a Stone Wall *85*
Small Plants and Stones *85*
8. **Gardens for the Backs of Houses** *87*
The Comma Garden *87*
9. **Gardens Close to Houses** *89*
A Stone Group Entitled "Waves Striking the Stones" *89*
Garden in Front of a Semi-basement *91*
Bamboo Grove with a Ritual Water Basin *92*
10. **Gardens on Concrete** *92*
Flood Tide in the Harbor *92*
The Depths of a Canyon *95*
11. **Courtyard Gardens** *97*
Miscanthus and Miscellaneous Trees *97*
12. **Gardens for Rooftops, Interiors, and Spaces under Floors** *99*
Sporting Seals *99*
Garden with a Flume *100*
A Stone Group Representing Friendship *101*
Japanese-style Rooms and Gardens in a Reinforced-concrete, Western-style
    Building *101*
Garden Beside a Sunken Parking Lot *111*
13. **Gardens for the Far North and for the Highlands** *111*
14. **Gardens for Hot Climates, Deserts, and Seaside Regions** *112*
15. **Garden by the Beach** *113*

III. Constructing a Japanese Garden *114*

1. **Apportionments and General Layout** *114*
2. **Planting** *115*
A. Transplanting Times *115*
B. Tree Roots *115*
C. Preparing, Raising, Wrapping Roots, and Pruning *117*
    Nemawashi *117*
    Raising the Tree *118*
    Tying and Wrapping the Roots *118*
    Pruning *119*
D. Transporting *120*
E. Planting *120*
F. Props *122*
G. Watering *122*

3. **Arranging and Constructing Stone Groups** *123*
  A. Setting One Stone *123*
  B. Grouping Several Stones *126*
     Visual and Spatial Construction *126*
     Visual Balance *128*
     Principle and Subordinate, Pursuer and Pursued *128*
     Opposition and Response *129*
     Proportions *129*
     Rhythm *130*
  C. Moving Stones into Place *132*
     Rubble-work Retaining Walls *134*
     Informal Tortoise-shell Pattern Wall *135*
     Standing-screen Stone Wall *135*
     Level Masonry *136*
  D. Construction Order *137*
  E. Stone Steps *137*
  F. Stepping Stones *138*
  G. Paving Stones *140*
4. **Constructing a Stream** *142*
5. **Constructing a Pond** *144*
6. **Setting Stone Lanterns and Towers** *146*
     Lantern Types *149*
     Tower Types *151*
7. **Setting the Ritual Water Basin** *152*
     Styles of Ritual Water Basins *154*
     Flumes and *Sozu* *155*
8. **Garden Paths and Staircases** *156*
9. **Bridges** *157*
10. **Patterns in Raked Gravel** *158*
11. **Fences and Gates** *159*
   Fences *159*
     Bamboo Tile Fence *159*
     Bamboo with Wide Braces *161*
     Fence of Unsplit Bamboo *161*
     Weir Fence *161*
     Korean Palisade *162*
     Open Palisade *162*
     Two-brace Open Fence *162*
   Partitioning Fence Sections (*Sodegaki*) *163*
     Bamboo Lattice Fence *163*
     Bamboo-blind Fence *163*
     Harp Fence *164*
     Bamboo Curtain *164*
     Broken Work Fences *164*
     Branch Fence *167*
     Charred Board Fence *167*
     Stone-plaque Fence *167*
     Folding-screen Fence *168*
   Gates *168*

Tree-branch Gate   *168*
Bow Gate   *169*
Diagonal Bamboo Gate   *169*
Zigzag Gate   *170*

Index   *171*

I
Characteristics of the Japanese Garden

1. Subdued, Subtle, and Elegant

Although some consider it completely in terms of form while others say that because of its Zen origins it is too profound and exalted to be accessible to the common man, the Japanese garden, in fact, belongs to neither category to the exclusion of the other. The role of Zen devotees in the development of the Japanese garden is confined to the creation of a refined—*shibusa*—style that offers recluse from the detested complexities of ordinary life. From their earliest history devoted to somber, elegant gardens rather than to gorgeous, ornamental ones, the Japanese people have long been fond of bringing home from mountains and fields plants and grasses to set out in the fronts of their houses in what was called a *senzai*, or garden plot in front of the front yard. With passing ages, the taste for simplicity gradually deepened to become what is called today *wabi*, a gentle, somber kind of beauty. Not limited to the followers of the Zen sect, the appreciation for the refined and subdued extended to all Japanese people.

Though most national groups to some extent exhibit characteristic attitudes toward color and form in gardens, it is scarcely to be wondered that Japan, an island country for centuries isolated from the rest of the world, should have created unique gardens as well as distinctive literature and art.

An inherent appreciation of the *shibusa*, reflected in a fondness for rural cottages and ivy-covered walls, enabled the peoples of the West to comprehend the beauty of Japanese gardens, but veiling in somberness and even melancholy gardens with streams and fountains or those with many flowers and trees, which in Western eyes should be allowed to retain their natural splendor, remains an exclusively Japanese tendency. The subtlety of concealing what is in itself gorgeous plays a vital role in the Noh drama and is so important to Japanese gardening that no garden lacking the veil of mystic refinement is considered truly beautiful.

To clarify my meaning, I will give a few examples. Japanese lacquerware, so well known in the West that it is sometimes called "japan," is more highly valued if its dazzling bright surface has been dulled to a calm, matted finish, corresponding to the subtle, mystic element in Japanese gardens. Put more plainly, though the charms of a naked dancing girl are apparent, a completely clothed woman can sometimes be equally provocative. The female impersonators of the Kabuki are a good example, but more refined and subtle are the actors of the Noh, who symbolize the female in performances suggesting the softened surface of treasured mat-finished lacquer.

Beautiful stones with glittering polished surfaces produce an effect aesthetically similar to that of a naked dancing girl, whereas the reds and blues of the surface of a stone weathered by countless ages of wind and rain and covered with moss are draped in a veil of mystical loveliness cast by Nature herself. Further concealing the gentle loveliness of such stones in the foliage of trees and in grasses weaves the spell of mystery essential to Japanese gardens.

In general, three aesthetic terms apply to the gradations of depth of refinement in gardens: sómber, subtle, and elegant. The somber beauty of *wabi* results from a thorough application of the principles of *shibusa*: the subtle and mystic arise when showy and gorgeous elements are partly concealed by a veil of mystery. Certain elements in Japanese gardens, however, though completely exposed, never become flashy, but fall somewhere midway between splendor and somberness. These last elements, which I call elegant, include lattices and windows with bamboo dividers and many kinds of plants, rushes, and areas of swept sand in gardens where simple shapes and colors are prized.

Tea gardens—sometimes called *roji*—emphasize subdued beauty; gardens employing groves, springs or ponds as well as rock groupings, make wide use of subtle elements; and courtyard and passageway gardens tend toward the elegant.

2. Symbolization

Although stone placements and structural methods often merely suggest natural landscapes, they are sometimes symbolic evocations of mood or atmosphere. For instance, a rock that is neither tall, slender and pointed nor low and spreading but that is well proportioned and stands firm on the ground gives the impression of a neutral harmony of all thirteen of Franklin's virtues. The ability to set stones so that they symbolize human concepts helps, in the words of the Japanese proverb, "put the heart in order." More than an abstract art of instinct, emotion, and beautiful forms, symbolic rock grouping requires the evolution and expression of a concept of the ideal human. This idea is the main current of traditional Japanese gardening art and the basis of garden rock grouping.

In addition to concepts, rock arrangements can also suggest the moods of mountain or seaside through abbreviations employing only a few stones and plants. Shortening for effect plays an important part in several Japanese arts. The Noh actor represents a trip of many miles with a few steps and evokes a vision of water on a perfectly dry stage through words and actions. Though most Japanese poetry is brief by Western standards, the haiku, an extreme case of terseness, demands that the poet pack into each word and phrase rich visual and emotional symbolism. His words must resemble the iceberg in that they suggest great depth though apparently slight in volume. Similarly, in cramped garden spaces, each tree and rock must stand for much more than itself. To accomplish this, garden rock groups must emphasize Nature, artificiality must be supressed, and stones must be set to look as if they themselves wanted to be where they are, not as if some person arbitrarily put them there. A subjective symbolism will not necessarily produce on the viewer the idea held by the gardener. An untrained person no more comprehends the joys and sorrows latent in great music than a horse understands the Lotus Sutra, and a person with absolutely no knowledge of Japanese gardens cannot hope to appreciate their symbols.

Although idea symbols, the most subjective of all, require the viewer to have some notion of the thoughts held by the gardener, mood and atmosphere symbols appeal more generally. For instance, most people experience a feeling of sublimity on viewing the Yosemite crags or one of vastness on seeing the rock layers of the Grand Canyon. Similarly, rushes planted in a garden evoke the presence of water just as mountain plants do a sense of the highlands. On the other hand, visions of gods or of the creation of the crust of the Earth in such garden arrangements depend entirely on the conceptual and religious background of the person imagining such symbolism and will, in all likelihood, fail to communicate to a person of different cultural associations. If Japanese gardens were understandable only to the gardener who designed them or to one or two other people, they would never have won the hearts of countless people all over the world. They have done so, however, because, reserving concept symbolization and associational content for special occasions, they concentrate on mood and atmosphere symbols.

Since, in contrast to Western gardens, where plants are often used for symbolic purposes, Japanese gardens are distinguished by their use of stones, a few explanatory examples will be of assistance in understanding them better.

A standing stone (Fig. 1) is taller than the length of its diameter at the point where it enters the ground. The center of the section taken at ground level must connect with the center of the top in a straight line (main axis) perpendicular to the ground. Should the diameter at the ground level be equal to the height, the height will appear greater. For this reason I term "standing stones" only those whose heights are greater than their diameters. When the height is less, though the grain is vertical, the stone belongs to the "lying-down" category. When the height is greater but the main axis is inclined from the true perpendicular, the stone is an inclining (or peeping) stone (Fig. 2).

Some such stones have rough surfaces, whereas others are smooth. The stone in Fig. 1, more than twice as tall as it is wide and representing strength and

1. *Standing stone.*

2. *Inclining stone.*

3. *A calm standing stone and a peeping stone with a flat top.*

4. *A placid inclining stone.*

5. *A peeping stone with a flat top.*

6. *Round, cut stone with a flat top and a stone with a shelf-like projection.*

7. *Stone with force directed to the right.*

inflexible determination, might be compared to Napoleon or Alexander the Great, but the one in Fig. 3, about 1.5 times as tall as it is wide, suggests the sort of warmth in authority that is associated with George Washington or Abraham Lincoln. Stones of this kind are often selected to be the chief piece in a garden group. A flat top accentuates the peaceful mood of the symbol, but as long as the height-diameter ratio remains 1 : 1 or 1 : 1.5, even if the top is pointed, the stone will not seem too severe. Used to suggest sternness, the stones like that in Fig. 1 often emphasize the austerity of garden waterfall or evokes the feeling of precipitous mountains. Japanese gardens, however, always avoid sharply pointed rocks because they symbolize threats and evoke images reminiscent of the autocrats of the Reign of Terror. They are unsuitable for most garden purposes.

Some inclining stones suggest brave, reliable spirits, like valiant heroes, whereas others with flat tops, like that of Fig. 4, evoke the kind of love and warmth associated with the Virgin Mary. The flat-top peeping stone in Fig. 5, apparently maintaining calm within turbulence, reminds one of the brave man

8. A stone with its force directed to the left.

9. Two stones that, though physically separated, are deeply connected.

10. A skillful combination of lines of force.

who never loses his equipoise and is suitable to the symbolic representation of precipices where stability persists in the midst of thrilling action. Round, cut stones with flat tops (Fig. 6) suggest placidity.

When the main axis is either perpendicular or parallel to the ground, a mood of calm results, but when it inclines (Figs. 7, 8, and 9), motion is generated in the directions indicated by the arrows in the photographs. Because their forces move in one direction or another, these stones symbolize activity. By "force" I mean the possibility of movement suggested by a stone's incline to right (Fig. 7) or left (Fig. 8). To concentrate or oppose the movement of a single stone, it is essential to create a compact stone group by placing one or more accessory stones apart from, but related to, the principle stone. The straight standing stone and the stone directing its force to the left in Fig. 9, though separated by a small distance, maintain a close relationship. The connection between them is equally as intense as that between the stones in Fig. 3, whose forces connect at right angles. Fig. 10 shows a compactly organized group of six stones, in which the right- and left-directed forces of the smaller members create firm links with the two perpendicular ones.

3. The Somber Refinement of the Tea Garden

The teahouse is a place where friends meet in complete trust to drink green tea, take a light meal, and discuss things together. The tea garden brings solace and calm to the spirit both before entering the teahouse and upon leaving it when the ceremony has ended; it is called either the tea garden (*cha-niwa*) or the dewy ground (*roji*). The host of the tea ceremony is called the *teishu* or the *ta;* his assitant is called the *hantō*, and his guests are the *kyaku*.

Refined, calm, beauty (*shibusa*)—lately the subject of much interest in the West—finds its most thorough expression in the Japanese tea garden, generally divided into two sections, the inner and outer *roji*, but sometimes expanded by the addition of a mid-*roji*. The inner *roji* emphasizes the atmosphere of *shibusa;* and it is to that area that the term "tea garden" most often refers.

The joy of the tea ceremony appeals to people sated with gorgeous things and longing for simple refinement, much as a fresh salad tempts the palate of a man who has just eaten a thick, juicy steak. The name of the light food served at the tea ceremony, *kaiseki*, has an interesting derivation. It originally referred to a warmed stone (*onjaku*) slipped inside the kimono on cold days to ward off chill, but it later acquired the meaning of a light meal adequate only to stave the sharpest pangs of hunger, as a warm stone next to the stomach creates the illusion of one's having eaten a little food. For this reason light, fresh foods are most highly valued for tea ceremonies.

The word *shibusa*—actually connected with the palate and meaning bitter— when converted into emotional terms becomes *sabi* and *wabi*, both meaning a serene melancholy. Liberated for a period from the confusions and demands of daily society, the host and his guests consciously reflect in calm upon themselves and enjoy the pleasing sadness that pervades their hearts as they do so. I am sure that people of culture everywhere, whether interested in or indifferent to the Japanese tea ceremony, have experienced similar emotional states: sincerity, trust, friendship, and reflection know no bounds of past, present, East, or West. The purest meaning of the tea ceremony consists in just these feelings; it is not a chance for the master to show off his fine porcelains, for the wife and daughter of the house to display their richest clothes, or for the tea master to exhibit his skills in the various formal moves of the ceremony. Its true significance arises from the sincere reflections on the meaning of life, thoughts shared in quietude by a group of friends; and it is the essential duty of the tea garden to create an atmosphere suitable to such reflections. Flashy stones, and fussy stone lanterns introduce notes of vainglory, lust for power, greed, and the disorder of the commercial world. Trees bearing large red or pink flowers are to be avoided in favor of wind- or insect-pollinated plants with small white or pale lavendar blooms. Furthermore, the flowers in the *tokonoma* alcove inside the teahouse must never exceed a single branch with one or two blossoms and, though obviously an ornament, must underscore the general mood of somber sadness. By their limited number they should concentrate the spirit of the viewer on the quiet elegance of the occasion instead of attempting to compete with the flowers of the garden.

Tea-garden stones should be chosen for dark colors and the ease with which mosses grow on them, not for the beauty of reds, blues, and whites, or for the dramatic effect of roughened surfaces. Elaborate ornamental stones may be set in the outer *roji* or in gardens visible through the open windows of the tea-house, when moon viewing is the aim of the ceremony, but they should be excluded from the more refined inner *roji*.

Stone lanterns should be small (from three to five feet tall), should lack base stones, and should be moderate and unassuming in form. Since fountains tend to suggest luxury and glamour, they are unsuitable, but a small trickle of water into the ritual stone water basin, a gentle overflow from such a basin or from a well crib, the quiet dripping of water from a bamboo flume, a slowly flowing stream about one or two feet wide, or a small surface of water shaded by trees and reflecting the light from a lantern contribute to the *shibusa* of the mood.

The most important element in the tea garden, the ritual wash basin (*tsukubai chozubachi*) is the place where, before entering the teahouse, the guest rinses his hands and mouth in token of his desire to cleanse his spirit of all worldly stains. The act resembles the gesture of placing the palms together in a prayerful attitude before the Shinto gods or the Buddhist deities or the Christian symbol of making a sign of the cross on the chest. In fact, the *chozubachi* is itself an extension of the Japanese custom of washing the hands to cleanse the spirit after going to the toilet or of rinsing them of wickedness before making a pilgrimage to a Shinto shrine.

Regarding the teahouse precincts as, in a sense, holy, the tea master, in feudal times, provided racks outside the building where samurai were obliged to leave their swords; no weapons were permitted inside. The *tsukubai chozubachi*, similarly, offers the guest a place to cleanse himself of wickeness, selfishness, or violence, which jar against the atmosphere of mutual trust and friendliness of the ceremony.

The trash hole (*chiri ana*) under the eaves of the teahouse serves a similar purpose because it reminds the guest to discard any rubbish that might be cluttering his spirit. The hole, needless to say, is not intended as a receptacle for wastepaper; its function is symbolic. Though it might appear strange to the eyes of a Westerner, this tea-garden custom belongs to the same tradition as the belief that correctly arranging stone groups cultivates a proper spirit.

Second in importance to the ritual water basin are the stones on which one walks through the tea garden. Whether stepping stones (*tobi ishi*) or paving (*tatami ishi*), they always prevent damage to the moss covering the ground and indicate where one may walk. A fist-sized stone, called a *sekimori ishi*, placed on top of one of the stepping stones cautions the pedestrian to proceed no farther. Named for guards (*mori*) posted at certain boundaries (*seki*) in cities during the feudal period, this stone tells much about the traditional Japanese character. There is no reason why a person could not kick the stone aside and continue, just as long ago there was nothing to prevent guests in inns from unlawfully entering the rooms of other guests when only sliding paper doors partitioned one from the other. But the old attitude was to accept responsibility for one's actions and to abide by such established codes as that reflected in the *sekimori ishi*. However, things have changed in Japan, and today every front door is locked against intruders. In addition to their purely physical importance, by directing the attention to the path, stepping stones inspire spiritual unity.

Although few houses in the West include a separate teahouse and tea garden, using the ideas represented by them in parts of gardens is relatively easy.

Since the quiet, somber mood of the tea garden requires dark places where grass will not grow, it makes good use of dim, northern sections or of places shaded by neighboring houses.

Under my direction, Akira Ohira, with the assistance of local gardeners, built a Japanese teahouse and garden for the Swiss Pines Park in Philadelphia, operated by Mr. Arnold Bartschi. The fence and gate in the chart in Fig. 11 mark the boundary of the tea garden; the waiting pavilion is in the outer *roji*, and the teahouse is in the inner *roji*. As I explain the garden, beginning with the inner *roji*, the reader will find it helpful to refer frequently to the placements of the various elements in Fig. 11.

The ritual wash basin (Fig. 14) by itself can introduce the feeling of the tea garden into very cramped spaces. The stone in front, called the front stone (*mae ishi*), provides a place to squat when using the basin. The stone on the left, partly concealed by *Pieris Japonica*, is called the candle stone (*teshoku ishi*) because, during night tea ceremonies, the host places a candle there while the guest rinses his hands. The stone on the right is called the hot-water-bucket stone (*yuoke ishi*) because, in winter, the host puts a bucket of that liquid there so that guests can warm the water in the basin for greater comfort. The measurements for these stones appear in Fig. 13. The edge of the water hole in the basin should be about two feet from the near edge of the front stone, and a person squatting on the front stone should be able to reach the candle stone with his left hand and the hot-water-bucket stone with his right. If the front stone is set about one or two inches higher than ground level and the water surface in the basin is from six to ten inches above the ground, the candle stone's height should be mid-way between these two, and that of the hot-water-bucket stone should be about halfway between those of the front stone and the top of the hot-water-bucket stone.

These sizes are standards, but other arrangements are possible. For instance, the front stone could be set lower than, or even as much as a few steps below, the stepping stones, in a style called an *ori-tsukubai*; or the basin itself might be of several different types: the *fusen* type (Fig. 259-D) or the taller *shiogama* (Fig. 259-G). In these cases, the heights of the candle, hot-water-bucket, and front stones must be adjusted to that of the basin. Although lowering the height of the hot-water-bucket stone makes little difference to its function, lowering

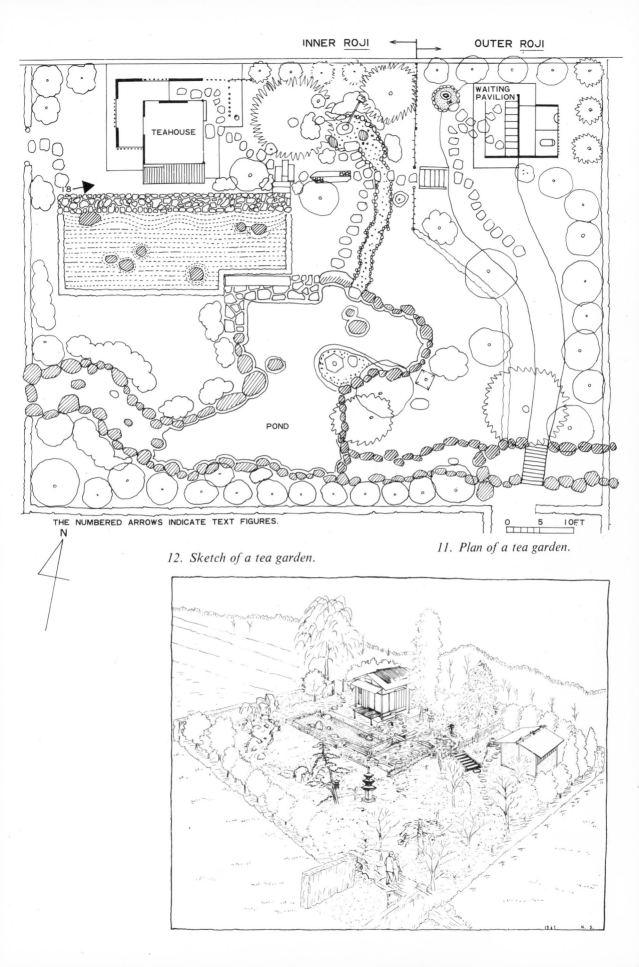

TEAHOUSE

WAITING PAVILION

POND

THE NUMBERED ARROWS INDICATE TEXT FIGURES.

N

0   5   10 FT

12. Sketch of a tea garden.

11. Plan of a tea garden.

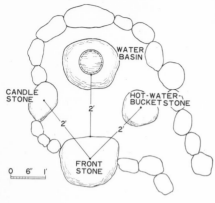

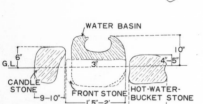

14. *A tea garden ritual water basin.*

13. *Measurements for a ritual water basin.*

the candle stone could spoil the lighting. The important thing is to create a balance among all the stones and to allow them to fulfill their functions efficiently. All these stones are called *yakuishi*, or stones that have roles to play.

In front of the basin is a depression with a drainage opening, concealed by rocks, to carry off the water that overflows the basin's rim. The depression, called the "sea," should be from seven inches to one foot in depth. Shallower than that, it looks unpleasant, deeper, it arouses feelings of anxiety in the person using the basin (see dimensions in Fig. 13). It should have a concrete bottom, a central hole (about one inch in diameter), and an inclined groove for the water flow. The water from the flume should drip slowly, rather than flow continuously. As the poem by the great monk-poet Saigyo puts it:

A house where the crystal water, not flowing,
    falls drop by drop among the moss-grown boulders.

The area around the ritual water basin is usually covered with moss, but for areas of the world lacking this plant, I recommend *Arenaria* sandwort, which, though less subtly refined than good moss, is interesting because of its small white flowers.

I shall now explain the order guests follow in entering the teahouse because understanding it helps in appreciating the garden itself.

Guests first proceed to the waiting pavilion where they sit drinking a warm brew called *kōsen* as they await the host, who soon emerges from the preparations room (*mizuya*), greets the first guest, who leaves the pavilion for this purpose, then returns to the preparations room. The first guest goes back into the waiting pavilion and, after about as much time as it takes to smoke a cigarette, once again goes out and enters the inner *roji*. Leaving a few paces open from person to person, all the other guests follow. When the first guest stops in front of the ritual water basin, all of the others halt and await their turns. The order in using the water basin is unimportant, but the following is standard.

The guest lifts the dipper from the basin in his right hand and pours water over his left. He then takes the dipper in his left hand and pours water over his right hand. Having done this, he once again takes the dipper in his right hand, fills it with water, pours the water into his left hand, and fills his mouth. After he empties the water from his mouth into the depression in front of the basin, he fills the dipper again, holds it up so that the water runs downward and washes the handle, and returns it to its position on the basin. Generally the bowl of the dipper should be on the left, but if the host, by mistake, has set it the wrong way, it should be returned to the position in which he put it. To correct his placement is considered rude. When this is finished, the first guest, admiring the garden as he goes, proceeds to the teahouse; the other guests move one by one to the ritual water basin.

The combination of paving stones and long rectangular stones (*tanzaku ishi*) in Fig. 15 solves the problem of a sloping approach to the teahouse. The staircase that was formerly used here was out of keeping with the tea-garden mood. The low plants around the *tanzaku* stones are *Pachysandra terminalis* and fern. Such plants are often used to fill in around the edges of stones and at the bases of other plants lacking low-hanging branches. When so used they are called *nejime*. It is wise to avoid gaudy flowering plants like the azalea in the inner *roji*.

As the guest approaches the teahouse, he sees under its eaves the *chiri-ana* (Fig. 16), which reminds him to remove all worldly stain and unclean thoughts

15. (*left*) *Stepping stones from a ritual water basin to a tea garden.*

16. (*right*) Chiri-ana.

from his heart so that he can enter the teahouse in the spirit of true friendship.

The traditional entrance to the tea house, the *nijiriguchi*, is so low that guests must crawl into the room. In front of the *nijiriguchi* is a large stepping stone called the *nijiriagari fumidan-ishi*, or the platform on which one steps before entering the *nijiriguchi* (Fig. 17). Usually placed about five inches from the foundation of the building, the *nijiriagari fumidan-ishi* should be from one foot to one foot and three inches lower than the sill of the *nijiriguchi*. To enter, the guest places his fan on the floor on right side of the entrance, parallel with the sill, looks into the room to ascertain the placement of the hearth and *tokonoma alcove*, picks up his fan, and crouching, enters the room. Remaining in a kneeling position he adjusts his footwear beside the stepping stone, puts his fan in front of him, and with both hands on the floor, admires the hanging scroll in the *tokonoma*. If it is calligraphy, he reads it from top to bottom; if it is a painting, he looks at it from the bottom to the top. Still kneeling, he takes his fan in his hand, then stands and moves to the hearth where, after putting his fan down in front of him again, he examines the carefully arranged charcoal fire and the kettle used for heating water. He then moves to his own place. All of the other guests, entering one by one, go through the same procedure, and the last man to come in, called the *otsume*, quietly pulls the sliding door of the *nijiriguchi* till it is from four to five inches from being completely shut. He then bangs it closed with a loud noise that signifies the readiness of the guests. The host then emerges and greets the gathering.

If the garden is to provide a pleasing vista as well as a pathway to the teahouse, it is possible to leave some window or door in the building open. In cases like this, either a stone-group and sand garden or a fountain and pond garden make a good substitute for the traditional tea garden. The teahouse illustrated here has a wide wooden veranda (Fig. 18) with a sand-and-stone garden in front for effective moon viewing, but since it must sometimes be a part of a tea ceremony, large flowers or noisily gurgling fountains have been avoided.

17. Stone step before the traditional low, teahouse entrance, and stones inserted at the building foundation.

18. A teahouse veranda.

The lattice door (*kininguchi*) between the veranda and the *nijiriguchi* provides access to the tearoom for people of high social status (Fig. 12). But today, paying little attention to such distinctions, many tea masters have all the guests use this entrance and maintain the *nijiriguchi* as no more than a traditional formality.

Stones about the size of a fist, arranged flat top up under the edge of the building, lighten the effect of the teahouse foundation (Fig. 17). Called *sashi-ishi* and put in place after the building is completed, these stones either come in direct contact with the foundation, as in the photograph, or are from two to three inches lower. In most cases the tops form a straight line, but it is possible to create indentations, as long as balance is maintained.

The first thing to be discussed concerning the outer *roji* is the waiting pavilion. In the one in Fig. 19, the bench for the guests is clearly visible. The floor might be made of paving stones, concrete with granite gravel imbedded in it, or soil or concrete set with stepping stones connecting with those in the garden. Frequently, the line of stepping stones at the entrance to the waiting pavilion splits in two directions for a distance of two or three stones. Although, in the past, a special seat was designated for the main guest and others for the remaining guests, this custom is rarely followed today. In fact, in many instances, no waiting pavilion is provided; guests wait in the main house and proceed directly to the teahouse from there.

The stone called the host's stone and that called the main guest's stone from which the initial greetings are made are no more than two of the stepping stones in front of the waiting pavilion. It is unnecessary to set two different stones soley for this purpose.

In very polite ceremonies, the *hanto* (the host's assistant) opens the gate between the inner and outer *roji* and comes forward to greet the guests. He is also responsible for changing the water in the ritual water basin and for cleaning the garden and sprinkling it with water before the guests arrive and before they leave the teahouse.

Sprinkling water plays an important role in all Japanese gardens, but in the tea garden, the host must be specially careful to see that the trees, lanterns, stepping stones, moss, and the stone on which to remove footwear are thoroughly doused. The times appointed for sprinkling, the so-called three dews, are before the guests arrive, just before they leave the teahouse after the completion of the light *kaiseki* meal, and just before they leave for the last time after having drunk their tea. A gong sounds to tell the *hanto* when he must conduct the guests back to the teahouse when the intermediary recess has ended. The three dews and the three charcoals—the three times during the ceremony when charcoal is added to the fire—signify the host's respect for his guests.

If no *kakehi* flume is used to replenish the ritual basin, the *hanto* must change the water before the guests arrive and before they leave the teahouse. Since, reminiscent of mountain homes where bamboo pipes transport spring waters from distant places, the *kakehi* flume is attractive, many people prefer to use it.

As somber refinement must fill the inner *roji*, elegance must pervade the outer *roji*.

The toilet behind the waiting pavilion may be of two types: one intended for actual use (*kafuku setchin*) and one designed to be an ornament (*suna setchin* or *kazari setchin*). The one illustrated, though a *kafuku setchin*, is never used.

Finally, a special stone, called the *gakumino-ishi* placed just to the side of the

19. *A waiting pavilion.*

19-a. The entrance.

other stepping stones, permits the guest to see the carved plaque hanging in the teahouse eave, but it may be omitted and the ordinary stepping stones arranged to provide the same view.

Though the construction of a real tea garden involves many somewhat troublesome conventions, if the enjoyment of the tea-garden mood is all that is required, a five-foot square with a ritual water basin and a *kakehi* flume with the appropriate planting will suffice.

21. View toward the entrance from the gate.

4. The Elegance of the Alleyway Garden

The area designated "alleyway" serving largely for passage—from the house to the teahouse or from the gate to the front entrance—is usually too long and narrow for leisurely strolling and should, consequently, be simple and elegant.

I treated the long, narrow front garden in Fig. 20 as an alleyway space. Fig. 21 is a view from the gate, and Fig. 22, one from the entrance of the house. The planting is bamboo (*daimyochiku*) along the fence and some *Dendropanax trifidus* in the inner section. This together with the white (*Sakuragawa*) gravel and the single small stone produce an elegant effect. Using the rectangular *tanzaku* stones as paving lightens the total feeling. This idea is good for any passageway at the side of a house.

20. Plan of an alleyway garden.

22. View of the gate from the area in front of the entrance.

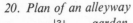

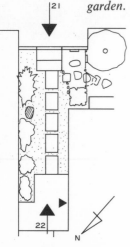

5. The Subtlety of a Garden with Pond or Fountain

The garden in Fig. 23 originally consisted of a thick stand of cryptomeria cedars. The trees left standing conceal the pond and though they would soften the effect, I avoided large ornamental stone groups because of the rural nature of the surroundings and have held the number of stones to a minimum. Had the cedars not already been on the land, I doubt that I would have thought of using them in this way.

In gardens of this kind, the pond should be as large as possible—as much as one-quarter of an acre—but even a smaller one, if concealed partly by a stand of trees, produces a satisfactorily subtle mood. Fig. 24 shows the left side of the pond viewed from the house, and Fig. 25, the right side.

Rising from a spring in the grove of cedars, the pond water drains off to the surrounding paddies for use in rice cultivation. Its constant flow, consequently, keeps the pond fresh and clean and enables the owner to raise carp.

When the surface of the water in a pond is roughly one-half inch lower than the surface of the ground, it gives the feeling of abundance, but when it is as much as five feet lower the steep surrounding wall of rocks inspires quiet and calm. Apart from gardens with fountains, the Japanese never employ water levels higher than the land. Furthermore, deep water is unessential because the charm of the pond is the reflection on its surface of clouds and trees and the ripples made by the wind. If large carp are to be kept the water should be about as deep as the fish are long. Generally, from one to two feet with a three-foot section is safe. Since the water near the surface of the pond is cleaner than that at the bottom, overflows should be arranged to siphon off the soiled part first. I will discuss pond construction later.

23. Plan of a garden with a pond and spring.

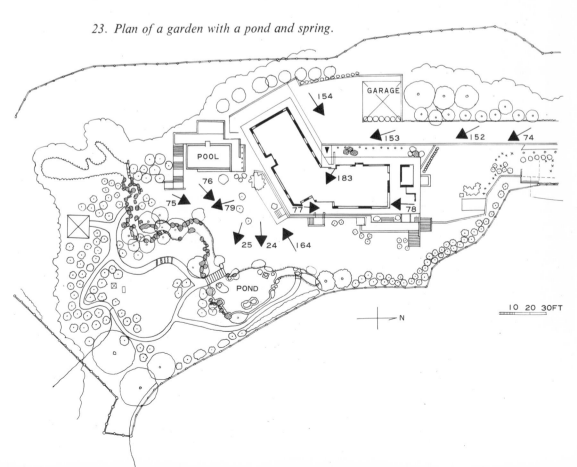

24. Left section of a garden with pond and spring.

25. Right section of the same garden.

6. The Symbolism of the Sand and Rock Garden

Through the use of vertical standing stones and flat areas of sand, the garden whose plan appears in Fig. 26, attempts to symbolize the mood of a still, deep river between steep banks. The peeping stones soften the stern aspect of the standing stone. In terms of height ratio, the standing stone on the right (Figs. 27 and 28) should be about a foot lower than it is and the one on the left and the small standing stone in the front of them about seven or eight inches lower. Nevertheless, slightly taller stones strengthen the symbolism created by the flat sand areas. Furthermore, keeping the height difference between the two standing stones very small, closes the sides of the composition and makes the stones resemble steep cliffs. In other words, in this case, the object of attention is not the standing stones but the space they demarcate.

The location, atop a hill in Kamakura, where the winds are often very strong, forbade the use of tall trees and limited the materials to stones, sand, and lawn. The stones are a beautiful green chlorite, and the silver firs planted by the standing stone on the right subtly shade the entire composition.

The combination of sand and grass does not glare in the sun as sand alone does.

Sand and stone arrangements are possible on top of concrete or in small indoor spaces because, they require no light and no water.

26. Plan of a garden composed of raked gravel and stone group.

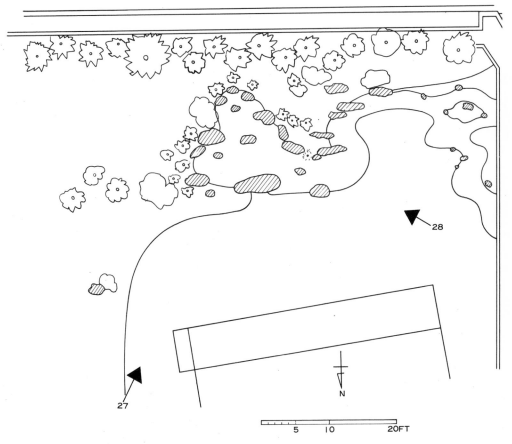

27. *View of a gravel and stone garden from the side where the house stands.*

28. *View from the right side of the garden.*

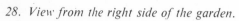

II
Japanese Garden Elements in Various Settings

1. Apportioning Space

When it is necessary to decide where in the domestic layout to include Japanese garden elements, first make provisions for the following essentials: entrance, exit, and passageway for the automobile, garage space, children's play area, storage, some grass, flowers, and trees. Insure sufficient space for the first three before doing anything else because they cannot be reduced beyond a fixed minimum—they also need not be expanded beyond a certain size. For a limited site, keep them as small as possible without interfering with their functional efficiency; use the remaining land for lawn, flowers and trees. For very cramped spaces, decide whether the Japanese garden will replace or incorporate the flowers, lawn, and trees, or whether it will be a small element in a generally Western layout. Of course, with more spacious gardens, even after allotting suitable area to all the other functions plus establishing lawn, flower, and tree spaces, it is often possible to add a complete Japanese garden wherever the owner wishes.

Japanese elements improve and beautify the passages and alleyways running beside houses.

The site illustrated by the plan in Fig. 29 (taken from *McCall's Garden Book*) is probably one of the smallest in the United States. In the compact plan, after allowances were made for car passage, play area, and garage, only a minimal amount of space remained for lawn and planting. Even I, a Japanese garden designer, could not agree to demolishing the limited lawn space for the sake of Japanese garden elements. If tall surrounding buildings spoil the lighting and ventilation so that grass will not grow, a Japanese sand and rock garden solves the problem, but a healthy lawn can easily be used in a modified Japanese style. For instance, at the inner edge of the lawn in Fig. 29, are two natural stones with plants around their bases to suggest the open fields. The third stone, on the left side of the garden, balances the other two. The curve in the walkway harmonizes with the total natural feeling. My general approach in this case was to use few flowers and two or three stones to symbolize the atmosphere of the wide plains. Should a Japanese stone lantern seem desirable, it might be set under the trees in the front garden with a flat-topped stone beside it. Traditionally stones so placed are to stand on when lighting the candle inside the light compartment, but aesthetically their horizontal lines contrast pleasingly with the verticals of the lantern.

Should the environment make raising good grass impossible, a sand and stone garden of the tea-garden style or one with a small stream might suit this small

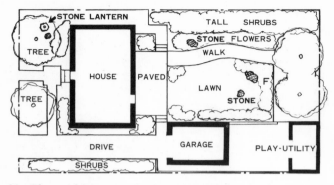

29. Plan and locations for Japanese gardens.

site admirably.

On the following pages I offer a number of Japanese gardens that, though constructed for the most part in Japan, could be used to advantage in the West because most of the homes to which they belong are in Western, or very nearly Western, architectural styles. It is important, however, to notice the sizes of the windows in the houses. When the Japanese first imported Western building styles, they used small European windows. These, however, later proving ill suited to the hot and humid Japanese summer, were replaced by large, Japanese-style sliding windows, which unite garden and interior. Consequently, the Japanese both go into the garden to admire the trees and plants and remaining seated inside, enjoy an ample view, comparable to what the Westerner sees from his terrace or veranda. For this reason, in planning gardens for the West, emphasis must fall on the appearance as seen from out of doors. I do not mean to imply, however, that differences in window size in any way restrict the application of Japanese garden elements. In fact, all Japanese gardens can be enjoyed from out of doors, and the spacious promenade gardens are so large that unless one goes into them and walks around, the rich variety of the planning goes unappreciated.

2. Gardens with Spacious Lawns

Lawns, though beautiful and charming by themselves, require space, light, and good ventilation. Japanese homes almost always surround their gardens with fences. In America, however, even when gardens are small, the general absence of fences opens wide areas for fine lawns. To satisfy the needs of the traditional Japanese and American methods, I have included some gardens, constructed under my supervision, which suggest ideas to both homeowners who surround their private gardens with fences and to those who use no partitioning between their own and neighboring areas.

A Lawn Garden Overlooking the Sea

Situated on a hill, the garden in Fig. 30, enjoys a view of the sea on the south across the rooftops of a town and through a grove of black pines. Hills closing in directly on the west and north and from a slightly greater distance on the east create a topographically ideal residential site. The only tall tree on the far side

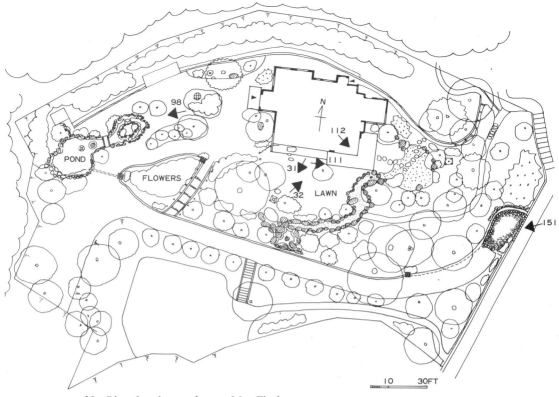

30. *Plan for the garden at Mr. F's home.*

of the lawn is a single pine (*Pinus pentaphylla*), and the sea is visible across the tops of the low (from two to three feet) azaleas, winter camellias, and *Enkianthus perulatus* at the edge of the flat expanse of green grass. Concealing part of the distant vista of the sea with the pine tree (Fig. 31) intensifies the beauty of the garden and creates a typically subtle Japanese mood. Contrary to the customary placement deep in a grove of trees, the stone lantern—a *koshin* type—produces a different effect because it stands boldly against the distant view. The National Railways Tokaido Line, which passes through the town at the foot of the hill, provides an interesting motion accent. Fig. 32 shows a view of the terrace and house from the garden.

31. *Lawn with the sea in the background.*

32. Flat area of lawn in front of the terrace.

The mountain on the east, about 200 yards from the house, is covered with chestnuts, zelkova, and oaks; to blend the garden with it and to provide a semi-obstructed view of its sloping sides, I planted red pines, maples, and plums. Wild birds come to sing and bathe in this eastern part of the garden, where I introduced a small stream fed by a mountain spring (like the one in Fig. 111) and spread white sand between the planted area and the house. Grass and moss create the patterns illustrated in Fig. 30. Whereas the garden is dry and bright on the south, the east area is calm and refreshed by the stream.

Lawn Visible through a Stand of Black Pines

Though facing a road on the east, the lot is surrounded by neighboring houses on the other three sides. To block sight lines into the house and to obscure the neighbors' houses as much as possible, I surrounded the garden with a tall hedge and high plants. Although ordinarily the lawn would be directly in front of the house, to enable the residents to admire the water and the carp swimming in the pond from indoors, I placed the pond close to the house, the grass area for golf practice or for a children's playground beyond the pond, and a screen of black pines between the two. The trees partly conceal the grass and the waterfall stone arrangement and plants in the distant end of the garden, where because of the veil of subtlety they provide, even flashy ornamental flowers or elaborate stone groups would seem elegant and refined.

Fig. 34 is a view through the front gate, and Fig. 35 a similar view with the gate open. Among the bamboo (*daimyochiku*) nestle two somber stones, and under the carport stands a stone lantern (*Oribe* type) with Sakuragawa gravel spread beneath it. Easy to create in a narrow passageway space, this sort of bright elegance matches the gate and the black lattice at the far end of the entrance. In the area between the carport and the back garden, round-trimmed boxwoods harmonize with the shape of the sculptured piece (Fig. 36).

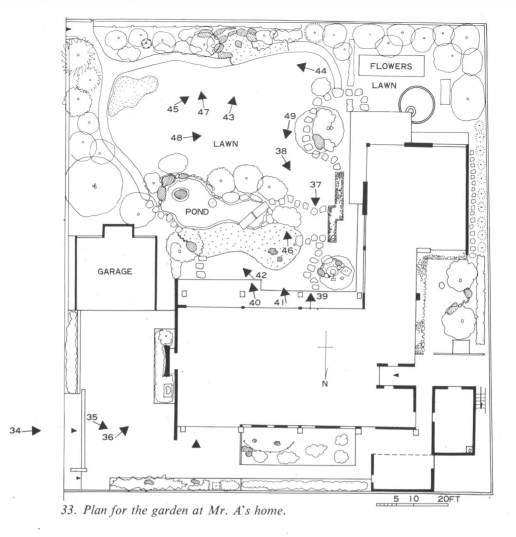

33. Plan for the garden at Mr. A's home.

34: View from the front gate.
35. Lattice separating the front and inner gardens.

36. *Pruned boxwoods and sculpture.*
37. *Lantern and ritual water basin in the inner garden.*
38. *Distant view of the corner with the water basin.*

39. Stepping stones and lawn in the right section of the garden.

In the right front corner of the inner garden (Fig. 37) I planted a pomegranate tree and set a boulder-shaped ritual water basin under it with a stone lantern (*mizuhotaru* type) beside it. Moss covers the ground, and *Dendropanax trifidus* completes the setting. This arrangement and the small stepping stones in front of it (Fig. 38) are for the tea ceremonies sometimes held in the house. Ferns planted at the base of the house help conceal the foundations. The paving stones on the right of Fig. 39 lead toward the crepe myrtle tree planted to hide the neighbors' house. Fig. 40 shows the right half of the pool in front of the house and the double stone bridge. A small stone bridge purchased for the purpose combined with another already on hand resulted in this double bridge, which is more interesting in this case than a single long one would have been. Though the pond, most of which is visible in Fig. 40, is small, the gravel beach

(*left to right*)
40. *Central pond and double bridge.*
41. *Pond with black pines.*
42. *Left side of the pond.*

43. *Lawn, the waterfall, and shrubbery.*
44. *Vicinity of the waterfall seen from the right.*

is spacious. It is made by setting small Ise pebbles (about one inch in diameter) close together in mortar. The base stones for the three legs of the lantern (*yukimi* type) are submerged; consequently, from one to two inches of the lantern legs are underwater. Stone groups ornament the area under the black pines and the pond itself. The stones, set after the concrete had been poured and the mortar finish applied, are held to the bottom and sides of the pond with mortar, which protects against water leakage. This method is important in ponds that are not constantly fed with fresh water. The standing stone under the red pine on the left side of the pond (Fig. 42) symbolically represents a steep precipice.

The stone lantern (*uzumasa* type) in the right of the inner part of the garden is buried to the top of the base in azaleas (*Pieris japonica*). To the left of it is a waterfall stone arrangement, over which no water falls ordinarily, but which is designed to function. Figs. 43 and 44 show the waterfall from the left and the right and illustrate how planting the shrubbery to lean toward the falls heightens the effect of the symbolism. The maple hanging downward into the falls further emphasizes the mood.

The golf practice area or children's playground in Fig. 46 is located between the black pines and the rear stones and planting. Moving the waterfall plants as far back as possible and making a small pond close to the house allowed plenty of lawn space.

45. *Lawn between the waterfall and the central planted area.*
46. *The same area seen from the opposite side.*

47. Stone lantern and plum tree in the left side of the garden.
48. Side section of the house and lawn viewed from the east.

49. View of the main house and lawn from the inner area of the garden.

I set a stone lantern (*Kasuga* type) and planted azaleas beside the plum tree in the left corner of the garden (Fig. 47). The path in front of the lantern leads to the back gate, which connects with a public road. Fig. 48 shows the lawn as seen from the east corner. The children's play area lies just behind the low hedge under the crepe myrtle. The view across the gate leading the house (Fig. 49) shows the white stone beach and the stepping stones to the double stone bridge over the pond. The azaleas (*Rhododendron indicum*) planted in front of the beach will require frequent pruning.

A Lawn Garden at the Base of a Cliff

The small lawn garden is at the base of the cliff on the north; neighbors' houses top both that and the cliff on the west. The site is open on the east and south to a view of the Tokyo surroundings, but since the buildings in the neighborhood are unsightly, the garden is planted to obscure them, to create a tiny lawn on the north, and to permit views of the bright city lights from the second story. Because the steep incline of the west side of the site forbids the planting of grass, after arranging a rock garden, and a small path for strolls among the trees and flowering plants there, I concentrated on the north section.

On the north too, to prevent landslides, I built a wall of natural stones and planted grasses and flowers among them to sugggest a rock garden. A traditional method of retaining sloping land in Japanese gardens is to set the stones so that they resemble a cliff that has fallen but is now stable. Because the lawn is on a higher level than the house, to handle drainage and for the sake of beauty,

50. A garden enclosed by an embankment.

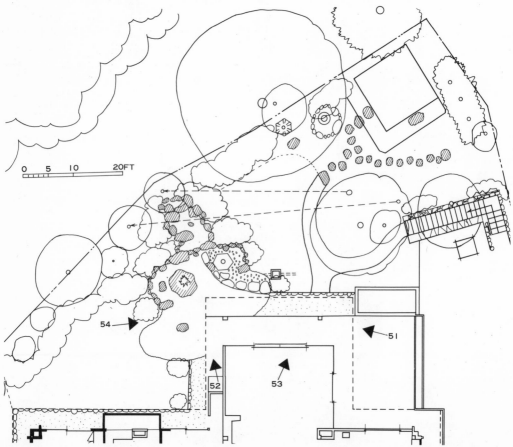

51. *Stone group at the bottom of the cliff and the pond at the edge of the terrace.*
52. *Rock island and a* yukimi-*style lantern.*

I placed a small pond at the edge of the terrace and ran a long, straight trench at the side of the pavement, from which it is possible to watch the fish swimming in the water (Fig. 51). The large stone set in the pond carries a crown of ferns and a small, but very old, black pine (Fig. 52). Fortunately, this stone is porous enough to provide the moisture the plants require for survival. Azaleas (*Rhododendron indicum*) surround the flat, stone-paved area at the pond's edge, where the stone lantern (*yukimi* type) stands. The pavement of flat stones

53. Sukiya-*style wing of the house and a section of lawn.*
54. *Sloping lawn and the trench pond.*

symbolizes a beach, and the edge stones are arranged for easy walking to make the pond accessible for cleaning.

   Although the owner of the house, a Cornell University graduate with fluent English, is so accustomed to the American way of living that his entire house is in the Western style, across the lawn he built a *sukiya*-style house (Fig. 53), where he treats his guests from abroad to the tea ceremony and Japanese food. Fig. 54 shows the slope leading to the *sukiya* house and the trough-like arm of the pond.

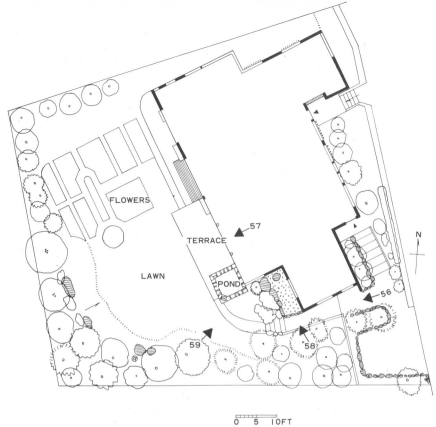

FLOWERS

TERRACE

LAWN

POND

57

56

58

59

N

0 5 10FT

55. Plan of the garden at Mr. M's house.

A Quiet Lawn Garden

Here, where there are no sea, cliffs, or traffic noise, I have used nothing but a flat lawn area surrounded by black pines and have avoided even streams and ponds, which would destory the calm effect desired. The owner of the house, another Cornell graduate who speaks fluent English, is one of Japan's most famous architects. Though not visible in Figs. 56 and 57, a low reclining stone to the right and a slight mounding of the ground at the bases of the pine trees provide all the variety needed.

56. Lawn seen from the entrance.

57. Lawn and black pines viewed from the living room.

58. Stones and gravel in an area one level lower than the garden.
59. Stone garden viewed from the lawn area.

A few steps at the entrance to the rear lawn garden provide transition between it and the front garden, which is about two feet lower. The area shown in Fig. 58, on approximately the same level as the front garden, is low for the sake of lighting in the work room adjacent to it. Though spread with Sakuragawa gravel and set with stones instead of being planted with grass, this part of the garden maintains a connection with the lawn garden by means of the large stone in the corner which is set at an angle with the house as if it were an extension of the retaining wall. The smaller stone beside it lies parallel with the first-floor veranda. Overflow water from the pond, bordered with rectangular stones, runs through the bamboo flume (Fig. 59) into the area below, where a drainage hole, concealed by gravel, carries it away.

A Garden Symbolizing Natural Fields

The entrance area (Fig. 60) and the hillock jutting forward create a curve in the drive to the front door and set the mountain-and-grove mood of the rear garden. Emphasizing natural shapes, I used no plants that require pruning and planted *Cornus Kousa*, *Carpinus laxiflora*, *Viburnum plicatum*, *Rhododendron Kaempferi*, *Rhododendron Albrechti*, and *Enkianthus perulatus*, brought in from nearby, around the slopes of a grass-covered hillock that continues to the eaves of the detached villa (Figs. 61, 62, 63), A rock garden around the terrace (Fig. 64) and a few steps leading into the garden solve the problem of height difference between the two areas. The dark stones under the planting next to the house are set in natural positions instead of aloof horizontals and verticals.

60. Front garden at the M residence.

61. Planting and lawn hillock near the house.
62. Left side of the hillock.

63. Detached wing of the house and the lawn.
64. Area in front of the main house.
65. Terrace steps.

66. *Planting and ornamental stones near a large building.*

An Open Lawn Garden

Next to a large memorial hall, I planted an open garden, of the type familiar to Americans, and accented it with a camphor tree (*Cinnamomum Camphora*), which, though too small for the building now, will soon grow to a suitable height. Then the gardeners can keep it as they want it by pruning frequently. Under it I set some large stones and planted round-trimmed *Pittosporum Tobira*.

Lawn That Is Also A Golf Training Course

In the mountains of Hakone, near the Sengokubara Golf Club (visible in the distance in Fig. 67), this mountain lodge garden doubles as a short golf course with tee, fairway, green, and area behind the green. Fig. 68 is a closer view of the ornamental stone pagoda in the garden, and Fig. 69 shows the lodge itself. The trees around the garden form a windbreak.

67. *Lawn area that doubles as a golf practice range.*
68. *Stone pagoda beyond the green.*

69. *View toward the lodge from the inner section of the garden.*

69-a. *View of the lodge from the pond on the right side.*

69-b. *View west from the bank of the pond.*

69-c. *Paving stones on the pond bank.*

A Golf Green in a Garden

Lacking the distant views of the Hakone Mountains available to the preceding garden, this one is shut in on all sides by the towering buildings of Tokyo. To block views from both the garden and the buildings, I planted tall shrubbery in the background and created an open practice green, which is always as carefully clipped as a real one. The small stream and rows of iris in the foreground of Fig. 70 separate the golf practice area from the rest of the garden. A path leads to the right to a pond and a teahouse with a pavilion. The path between the planting and the lawn—on the left in the photograph—leads beyond the green and behind the hill to a pond and a teahouse. The pavilion in the deep shrubbery on the left, ordinarily a pleasant resting spot, becomes a waiting pavilion on days when the master of the house holds a tea ceremony. Fig. 71 shows the view toward the house: Japanese-style rooms are on the left, and Western-style ones on the right. In the foreground is a golf practice bunker.

70. *Another lawn garden that serves as a golf green.*

70-a. *Stone lantern and the spring that is the source of the narrow stream flowing in front of the house.*

71. *View from the inner part of the garden.*

A Garden with Shrubbery Pruned in Mountain Shapes

High pruned shrubs spreading curving mountain-peak lines across the blue sky are lovely, but the yearly clipping they demand involves great work. The low (maximum four to five feet) azaleas (*Rhododendron lateritium* and *Rhododendron indicum*) are both easy to prune and beautiful when in blossom. The most important thing in planting shrubs to suggest mountains is creating a gentle, sloping foothill zone with lower plants—in this case, the azaleas. Leaving the taller trees unclipped adds interest. The small stream bed running in front of the azaleas is usually empty, but water allowed to flow through provides essential moisture in dry weather.

72. Lawn garden with shrubbery cut to suggest mountains.
73. View of the same area from the right side.

3. Gardens in Groves

People building new houses in wooded areas should always spare as many of the trees as possible if they want a grove-type garden. Although it is possible to bring in trees, they must be temporarily supported with unsightly props and they rarely develop the stately majesty of those whose roots spread wide in their own native soil. The gardener, on the other hand, frequently forced to import trees to unwooded areas, must use them as best he can to create the mood of a natural grove. Pine groves, cedar goves, and groves of miscellaneous trees each have individual personalities, but as long as their integrity is unviolated, it is perfectly all right to combine other plants with them.

A Garden in a Stand of Cryptomeria Cedars

This garden also appears in Figs. 23–25 and later in Figs. 152–154. A grove of straight, vertically rising trees imparts a feeling of solemnity to the entire garden. Although larger trees suggest sublimity, these moderate cryptomeria cedars control the entire scene with a unified feeling of sobriety. Using nothing but standing or flat-topped stones in this setting might seem a good idea, but in fact it would be tantamount to putting honey or sugar on a chocolate nut sundae. But just as a little something sour or salty enhances sweetness, so gentle curves or twisting streams intensify the natural mood of a grove of straight vertical

74. Part of the front garden of the MA residence.

75. View downward toward a garden in a grove of cryptomeria cedars.

trees. Slanting trees might also contribute to the atmosphere, but if too numerous they would destroy the feeling of a cedar grove.

Since an excessively dense stand of trees darkens the general tone and clouds the viewer's perception of the true depth of the garden, I transplanted most of the cedars from the vicinity of the house to lightly wooded areas and cut off the lower branches of the few remaining ones. Thus I provided good views through the trees of the utmost recesses of the garden, even of the distant ornamental pagoda in Fig. 79.

I brought the water from a spring bubbling out of the mountain in the depth of the garden to a waterfall where the pressure developed by the nine-foot land incline sends it pouring constantly into the pond. Maples hang over the waterfall, where rhododendron, *Pieris Japonica*, and ferns enrich the mood of the flowing spring water.

Around the small rest pavilion and under the cedars grow natural moss and bamboo grass to which I added bush clover, wild lilies, and other mountain plants.

76. *Pond seen through the cryptomeria cedars.*
77. *Cedars and the terrace.*

78. *Waterfall below the grove.*
79. *Closer view of the waterfall.*

Miscellaneous Trees with Black Pine

The design for the Hakone Rest Lodge of the Sankei Newspaper Company employs a natural stand of a number of different kinds of trees, including several black pines. Around the bases of these and of the *Cornus controversa*, spindle trees (*Euonymus Sieboldianus*), oaks, maples, chestnuts, and Hakone cherries, I planted low groups of azaleas (*Rhododendron dilatatum* and *Rhododendron Kaempferi*), *Pieris Japonica*, and *Enkianthus Perulatus*. Stones, in color and form resembling the lava-like boulders appearing here and there throughout the garden, are used as edging for the stream and pond. The stream (Fig. 81) which carries away drainage flowing onto the site from neighboring plots in heavy rains, becomes a small pond in front of the guest rooms and widens to a larger rivulet as it flows downward among natural and artificially set boulders and over a bed of small pebbles (Figs. 84–86). The flowing water and ponderous stones create attractive views from most of the rooms. The preceding illustrations show the pond and stream in construction; Figs. 89–93 show it completed and adorned with plants.

The intense shade from the many trees leads me to hope that moss will soon cover all the level areas, but for safety, on the slopes I have planted mountain grasses (in America, Kentucky Blue Grass would be fine). Grasses that are too bright and lush (*Zoisia Japonica* or the American bent grass) destroy the mood of a garden of this kind. I set the gravel on the slopes of the stream bed in mortar to prevent its being washed away in heavy rain and to facilitate scrubbing it with broom or brush. Although it takes a little more time, it is good to set the·gravel close together so that leaves dropping among the stones will not lodge there and make cleaning difficult. If set carefully and close, when seen from a distance, the stones will seem to rest naturally in the stream and will give no hint of being mortared in place.

80. Plan of the Sankei Newspaper Lodge at Hakone.

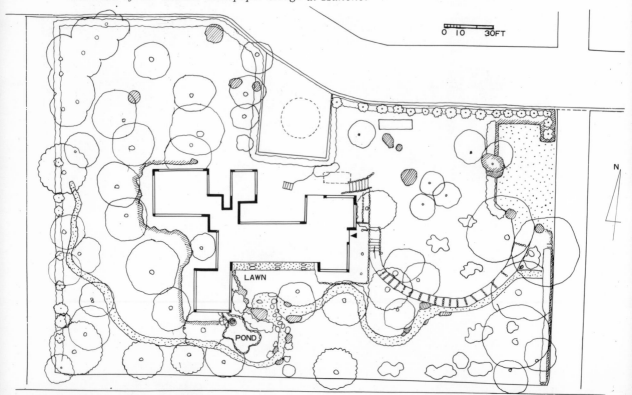

81. *Stream bed.*
82. *Digging holes in which to set the stones.*

83. *Setting stones leading to the pond in front of the guest house.*
84. *Mortaring the cracks in the stone group in front of the guest house.*

85. *The pond.*

86. *The stream flowing from the pond.*

Since a formal gate and fence would spoil the effect of a house in the forest, I used stones from the site to suggest a wall and a staircase flanked by two large boulders, also from the site, and obscured the boundary lines by planting local trees where a fence would normally be (Figs. 94 and 95).

87. *Applying mortar in which to set gravel.*

89. *Lower section of the pond.*
90. *View toward the upper section of the pond.*

88. *Setting the gravel.*

91. *Large exposed stone in front of the house. | 92. Retaining bank of the pond.*
93. *Stone group.*

94. *and 95. Natural stone boulders at the gate, and parking lot.*

A Garden in a Black-pine Grove

This garden, part of a new home, has mountains on the east and seashore on the south and west. To prevent strong winds from toppling the numerous black pines I had them closely pruned. Since these winds usually blow from one direction, all the pines incline the same way and thereby set the tone of the garden. To enliven the monotony of all pines I planted camellias and crepe myrtle and used such flowering shrubs as azaleas (*Rhododendron indicum* and *Rhododendron lateritium*), sweet daphne (*Daphne odora*), *Spiraea cantonensis*, *Spiraea Thunbergii*, *Kerria japonica*, and *Corylopsis pauciflora* around the bases of the trees and stones.

The blackish boulders with porous surfaces effectively tone down the too bright feeling of a garden containing only pine trees, but the result would have

96. Garden in a grove of black pines.

been displeasing had I used ornamental red, blue, or white stones instead. Black stones in a bright garden are always safe. A small spring supplies water for the pond (Fig. 96), but in such small quantity that I had the gravel pieces set in mortar at right angles to the water to force the flow to spread out over the entire bed. The skilful setting achieves the proper effect. Although it might seem more natural to simply rake unset gravel over the bed, water in small amounts flows under the stones and completely out of sight. The mortar solves this problem.

The water available is scarce but the convexities and concavities of the rocks

97. Waterfall in the same garden.

in the waterfall along the route of the stream are pleasing. Support rocks at the bases of the boulders impart a feeling of stability even to inclining stones. It is important to select a stone with a depression in the middle of the upper surface for the central element in the fall to force the water to flow always in a central course. Stones at the base of the fall that direct their force toward the water, as those in the illustration do, contribute greatly to the desired effect. They are called wave-dividing stones (*nami-wake ishi*). Though, seen isolated, the stone grouping seems jagged and confused, it assumes the correct calm when viewed through the boughs and trunks of the black pines. This is the element of subtlety I mentioned earlier.

Garden in a Grove of Miscellaneous Trees

The narrow pond in Fig. 98 is a part of the same garden that appears in Figs. 30–32. In this instance, by planting holly (*Illex serata*), azaleas (*Rhododendron dilatatum*), *Enkianthus perulatus*, witchhazel (*Hamamelis japonica*), *Viburnum plicatum*, weeping cherry, *Meratia praecox*, *Cercis chinensis*, and *Magnolia denudata* and by using gardenias (*Gardenia jasminoides*), *Rhododendron Albrechti*, and *Rhododendron japonicum* to conceal the water storage tank and the well, I managed to match the mood of the garden with that of the grove of miscellaneous trees instead of clearing the timber to make garden space.

Beyond the small stone bridge in Fig. 98, the narrow pond broadens and

98. Narrow pond in a grove of trees.

there, where the owners successfully breed fancy carp, I planted iris to harmonize with the small waterscape. A mountain spring keeps the pond supplied with ample fresh water. On the hill behind the pond, flower-laden wisteria vines reflect in the water. Actually a part of the front garden, this section can accommodate a small automobile in the narrow driveway on the left of the photograph, but a separate pedestrian path, passing through a tunnel of climbing roses, leads to the entrance of the house.

4. Gardens with Large Ponds

Ponds, even small ones, mirroring the sky, trees, sun, moon, and stars when they are calm, and sparkling with dancing light when ripples break their surfaces, have been called the eyes of the garden. Though artificial ones have their own loveliness, the beauty of a natural-style pond partakes of the grandeur of all nature. Some garden owners are so devoted to them that they construct large ponds which fill the greater parts of the sites.

A Bright Pond

Public roads pass the site on the north, east, and west, but since the south is open to the neighboring residence, I put the pond in the inner southern part of the garden where its location influenced it and made it bright and cheery. The

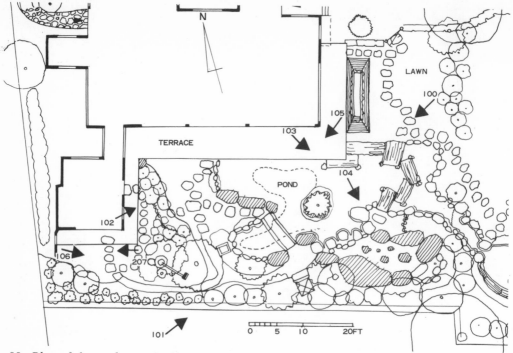

99. Plan of the garden at the FK residence.

house has wide glass doors and a terrace on the south side, and because the highway on the west slopes to the south, the garage is underground in the southwest corner; its top surface is part of the garden.

Though unsuited to the stone of the terrace, the wood and bamboo handrail became necessary after the child of the house nearly fell into the pond.

Black pines partially concealing the ornamental stone pagoda in Fig. 100 clearly illustrate the Japanese penchant for mysterious subtlety in gardens. A low pine (*Pinus pentaphylla*) ornaments the small island in the middle of the pond, and a zigzag stone bridge (*yatsu-bashi*) provides passage from one side to the other. In another section of the pond (Fig. 101), an earth-covered bridge performs a similar service. The stepping stones on the right lead to the zigzag bridge.

Ordinarily, lawn begins at terrace edge and leads to ponds in the distance, but the owner of this house, a pond devotee, requested a layout in which the

100. Pond and stone tower.

101. Earth bridge and island in the middle of the pond.

102. Pond comes in direct contact with the terrace.
103. Zigzag stone bridge.

104. *Waterfall at the upper reaches of the pond.*
105. *Teahouse in the distance.*

water actually extends a little distance beneath the edge of the terrace pavement (Fig. 102). Bamboo grass is planted under the small pine on the island.

Beyond the zigzag bridge (Fig. 103) a waterfall feeds the pond by means of a small stream. The close-up (Fig. 104) clearly shows the severe, craggy stones, seemingly hanging over the waterfall in a composition that is rugged but calm because of the flat tops of the stones. Maples adorn the perimeter of the waterfall group, whereas *Pieris japonica* conceals the bases of the stones and, with the help of ferns, fills in the crevices among them. The wave-dividing stone at the base of the falls splits the current of water and unifies the stone grouping by directing its force toward the waterfall. Should the group consist of as many as five wave-dividing stones, three of them must point toward the waterfall, though the other two may be directed elsewhere.

The small building in the right background (Fig. 105) is a teahouse, and the opening in its lower right corner is the ritual tea-ceremony entrance (*nijiriguchi*). Beyond that door is the kitchen used in the ceremonies. The ground under the birches that screen the teahouse is covered with moss, and the bases of the trees are hidden by *Pieris japonica*.

The tea garden in front of the teahouse (Fig. 106) contains a boulder-shaped ritual water basin and a stone lantern (*ariake* type). The stepping stones in the left foreground lead to the *nijiriguchi;* those on the right, to the entrance for personages of high rank. The stone lined and gravel spread gulley catches rainwater that falls from the eaves. *Ternstroemia japonica* and cryptomeria cedars conceal the water basin, moss covers the ground, and *Pieris japonica* and azaleas contribute to the general mountain-cottage mood.

106. *A tea garden.*

An Elegant Pond

The owner of this garden, like that of the preceding one, wished to bring the pond close to the terrace. Because I needed tall trees to obstruct the view into the garden from a neighboring tall building, I selected an image of quiet seclusion. Choosing trees demanded great care as thick evergreens result in gloom and melancholy, feelings to be strictly avoided when the aim of the garden is relaxation. I was able to draw the paper-thin line between seclusion and melancholy by rejecting evergreen oaks and similar heavy trees for lighter *Torreya nucifera*, and firs; *Chamaecyparis pisifera* and cypress would have been suitable too. The nine-story ornamental pagoda (Fig. 109) and the two-legged, cat's-paw stone lantern (*yukimi* style, Fig. 107) were chosen because of the lightness they impart to the total mood. The ordinary *yukimi* lantern which has three or four widely spread legs, would have been too airy for the image I had in mind.

Fig. 108, a view from the opposite side of the pond, clearly reveals the way the cypresses shade the pond and prevent its surface from reflecting the bright sky. To see a reflection of the blue above, one must step directly to the edge of the terrace. I arranged the planting this way to further emphasize the tone of seclusion and rest.

Since the family has no children, a handrail around the pond was unnecessary. Though the pond is somewhat dark, even when seen from the house, because the shadows of the trees seem to sink to its very bottom, the nature of the foliage saves the total effect from melancholy.

I wanted to use an ornamental Japanese rush and bamboo garden partition fence (*sodegaki*) at the place shown in Fig. 110, but since this is a passageway and since *sodegaki* are stationary, I compromised by using this hinged door that captures something of the traditional flavor.

107. Yukimi *stone lantern at the water's edge.*
108. *The same lantern and the house viewed from the opposite side of the pond.*

109. Nine-story stone tower in a small sequestered group of shrubbery.
110. Combination door and partition fence.

5. Gardens Combining Stone Groups and Gravel with Moss or Lawn

Traditionally, Japanese gardens combine symbolic stone and gravel groups with mosses, but lawn may be advantageously used. The cleanliness, color, and fine grains of gravel and sand are pleasing in themselves, but we Japanese most often use these materials to suggest bodies of water or ripples on water's surface.

Although in humid, cloudy areas—like Kyoto—white sand is beautiful, in drier, more sunny places its brilliance dazzles and hurts the eyes. In these areas, grayish, reddish, or brownish sands are preferable. Pure white sand always proves effective, however, in interior gardens, courtyard gardens, or any well shaded place.

A Stone Group with Half-concealed Mountains in the Background

The view in Fig. 111 is of the east side of the garden appearing in Figs. 30–32.

The mountains visible through the black pines, chestnuts, magnolias (*Magnolia kobus*), and zelkova trees, about 200 yards from the house, are the background for a hushed garden composition of stones and gravel.

The pink and white plums and the magnolias on either side of the stone pagoda set under the black pine tree add color to the wind-pollinated trees of the forest. In contrast to the winter-blooming plums, I set a pomegranate, which blooms in summer, in front of the stone tower; and by leaning it forward, I increased the sense of depth of the placement of the tower. I have used only one standing stone under the pomegranate and several inclining stones to balance the strong verticals of the trees. The base plants around the stones are azaleas (*Rhododendron indicum* and *Rhododendron lateritium*), and a single white-berry-bearing juniper is planted in the foreground to the right of the terrace in the illustration. White gravel covers the flat space, through which flows a narrow (one foot to two feet) stream fed by a mountain spring.

The twisted tree on the right in the view from the living room (Fig. 112) is a red maple of the kind often used in American gardens.

111. *Five-story stone pagoda in a garden of stones and raked gravel.*
112. *The same garden seen from the living room of the house.*

A Garden Called the Joys of Entering Nirvana

Although concept symbolization of the sort exemplified by this garden is highly subjective and may mean nothing to a person uninterested in such matters, I will give one example of my own approach to the representation of an idea that runs throughout Japanese classic literature from the Heian to the Edo periods, and from the romances of war, the *Tale of the Heike*, the *Hojo-ki*, and the *Tsurezuregusa*, to the *Joruri* plays of Chikamatsu Monzaemon, the *waka*-style poems of Saigyo, and the haiku of Bassho.

Fundamentally a Buddhist idea, the concept that the vantities of the world are passing and that only the joy of entering Nirvana has meaning finds popular expression in a poetic arrangement of the sounds of the Japanee syllabary. This poem, thought to have been written by the famous Shingon priest Kobo Daishi, says that fragrant colors always fade and that no one in this world can last for ever. Therefore, we should rise above this world to a plane where trivial dreams and distracting intoxications do not exist. A similar sentiment is expressed in lines from the Noh play *Miidera:* "The clouds of the five passions are dispelled, and we see the bright light of the moon of absolute reality." Both the poem and the lines from the play express the joy of entering the blessed state of

113. Garden entitled "The Joys of Entering Nirvana."
114. Central section of the garden seen from indoors.

115. *View from the left.*
116. *View from the right.*
117. *The veranda seen from the right.*

Nirvana, an idea that I have subjectively symbolized in this garden for the abbots
quarters at a Buddhist temple in Tokyo.

The large stone on the left in Fig. 114, a view of the stone group from the
abbot's quarters, symbolizes Amidha Buddha in his stability and perfect peace,
totally undisturbed by human ambitions and passions. The other stones, by
representing a variety of conditions and states—anger, sorrow, jealousy, delu-
sion, and attainment of Nirvana–are all directed in spirit toward Amidha and
thereby underscore the possibility of salvation for all beings. The photographs,
unfortunately, were made before planting was complete.

Fig. 115 is another view from the interior of the building; the large stone
on the left symbolizes Amidha. In contrast to this one from the left of the garden,
Fig. 116 is a view from the right side. Also taken from the right side but including a part of the veranda, Fig. 117 shows the bamboo flume which brings water
from the mountain in the rear to the stone water basin at the edge of the veranda.
I included water in the plan because I remembered a poem by a famous Sung-
period Chinese poet who said, "The voice of water brings rest to all."

To concentrate spiritual attention on the stone group, I decided to use only
moss, to avoid plants at the bases of the stones, and to spread the flat areas
with white gravel.

The hill behind and about ten feet higher than the garden is planted in a grove
of Moso bamboo with red pines, zelkova, and oaks in front. Although a natural
line boundary between the hill and the flat part of the garden would have been
possible, I chose the rustic wall of tortoise-shell-pattern masonry to avoid de-
tracting from the symbolic stones.

Using Sand to Symbolize a Calm Body of Water

Though the garden contains stone groupings and plants, the true protagonist is the flat area covered with grass and white Sakuragawa gravel representing a calm body of water. The plants in the background pruned to suggest distant mountains do no more than emphasize the flat space. Just recently planted, these shrubs have not yet attained the close density of foliage they will have in a few years. The serene Korean stone statue on the right in Fig. 119 harmonizes with the placidity of the whole.

The stone tablet at the entrance to the inner section of the garden (Fig. 120), also Korean, bears an inscription indicating the sympathy of an ancient Korean king for the labors of the farmers. The father of the owner of the house apparent-

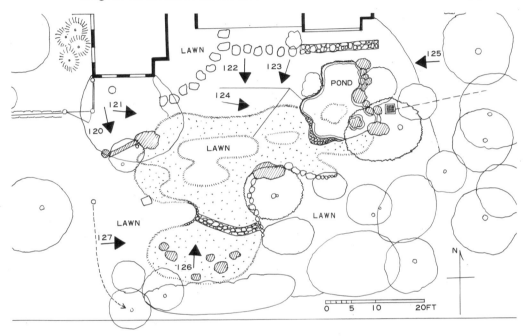

118. *Plan of the garden at the MO residence.*
119. *Sketch of the garden in Fig. 118.*

120. Entrance to the inner garden.
121. View of the left section of the garden from the gate.

ly grew very fond of China and Korea, where he lived for many years. The
path on the right leads into the inner garden. Fig. 121 is a view from the entrance
on the right side of the inner garden. In the foreground is a small island of
grass in the middle of white sand; in the left background is a small pond,
with a stand of trees beyond it. In Fig. 122, a view of the right half of the garden
from the living room area, the cloud-shaped island of grass and the sand area
highlight the relaxed mood of the plan. The large stone group and the moderate
and smaller sized ones in the inner section suggest seals at play in the water.
This mood becomes even more apparent with a comparison of this view to that
in Fig. 127. The Chinese black pines, camellias, and maples and the *Daphny-
phillum macropodum* and *Ligustrum japonicum* beyond them semi-conceal the
neighbor's house. The large juniper on the left, part of a previous garden,
was so interesting that, leaving it as it was, I made it the center of attention by
setting a large stone at its roots. Reeds planted between the grass and sand vary
the view. The stepping stones in the lower right lead from the entrance. The
view from the living room (Fig. 123) shows the juniper to good advantage.
Though not an old tree, it looks elderly and is neither haughty nor servile in tone.
The *Taxus cuspidata* half obscures and softens the large stone.

The scene in Fig. 124, directly in front of the reception room, consists of sand,
a beach set with small white stones, and a pond in which the owner of the house
raises brightly colored carp. The island in the gravel is planted with nothing but
charming phlox (*Phlox subulata*). The trees recently planted in the background,
include deciduous pomegranate and *Magnolia kobus* as well as evergreen firs.

The paved area in front of the reception room (Fig. 125) connects with the
stepping stones leading from the garden entrance. The edge of the pond is visible
on the left. The entire house was once Western in style, and the little structure
in the background in this picture was a detached Japanese-style pavilion. The
main house has, however, been rebuilt in Japanese style. Fig. 126 shows the
house. The juniper tree with the large rock in front of it is on the right. Fig.
127 shows the left part of the garden, where the path changes to paving stones
as it crosses the white gravel. The seal-like rock groups are also visible.

122. *View of the right section of the garden from the living room.*

123. *Central section of the garden viewed from the living room.*

124. *Left side of the garden in front of the reception room.*

125. *View of the garden entrance from the inner left section.*

126. *Inner section of the garden seen from the living room.*

127. *View of the left side of the garden.*

6. Gardens for Limited Spaces

In these cases I discuss gardens for sites lacking sufficient space, light, and ventilation for the cultivation of lawn. Although, in limited settings, growing trees over the years scrape their spreading boughs against the buildings around them, Japanese gardeners maintain natural and pleasing shapes and control sizes by careful pruning. Furthermore, even though it lacks light and fresh air, no space is so ill favored that gravel, stone groupings, and ritual water basins cannot work tasteful magic. Quite to the contrary, the subtle refinement of Japanese gardens and the symbolic elegance of stone groups often find fullest manifestation in small spaces.

A Garden with Rugged Stones

Though the house itself is large, only a small space is available between it and the neighboring building. I have pointed out in Figs. 21 and 22 ways to spread gravel and plant bamboo or *Dendropanax trifidus* for small gardens, but since the owner, who has a summer house in an area rich in rough textured stones, wanted to use them in a pond and waterfall arrangement, I followed his wishes. These volcanic rocks are easy to arrange tastefully when their grain can be set vertically or horizontally but much more difficult when the grains run at odd angles.

The pond and waterfall occupy the eastern half of the garden, on the south side of the building. The west half, though small, contains cryptomeria cedars, Japanese stewartia, and a certain amount of grass. A random arrangement of rocks and gravel on the east contrasts with the bamboo and white sand spread in front of the bath on the north side. Inside the entrance, in a small courtyard, bamboo and moss complement a single stone and some gravel.

As is seen in Fig. 129, the area in front and to the left of the entrance contains a boulder-shaped ritual water basin and a flume and is partially concealed from the reception room by means of a wattle fence section. Looking eastward from the entrance (Fig. 130), one sees the waterfall in the distance and water flowing from it into the pond. Stepping stones in the pond provide passage across its waters, and the small stones in the gravel beach are set to look as if the force of the flow from the waterfall carved the shore line. Usually placed at the edges

128 Plan of the garden at the O residence.

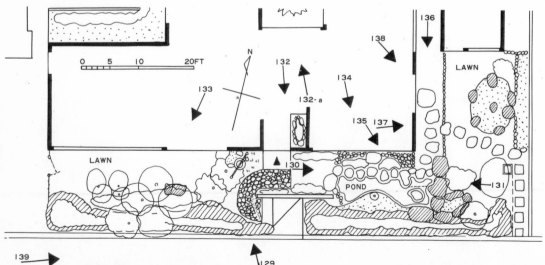

129. *Ritual water basin with a* kakehi.
130. *Small pond and a waterfall.*

131. *Stepping stones on the beach and in the water.*

132. Inside the entranceway.　　*132-a. Inner garden.*

*133. Stone masonry wall seen from the
    reception room.*
*134. Pond and stone group seen from the
    living room.*

135. *Waterfall stone group.*   136. *Left side of the waterfall.*

of beaches, as in the garden of the Katsura Detached Palace in Kyoto, this kind of stone lantern (*rakugan* style) symbolizes a famous scene in China.

The view from the east end toward the entrance (Fig. 131) clearly shows the stepping stones. The left side of the pond is arranged to suggest a natural crumbling cliff. Although it would have been possible to run the water all the way to the edge of the house, for the sake of piping I left a beach to hint that the waterline has receded because of evaporation.

Fig. 132 shows the inside of the entrance hall, where, because of the owner's fondness for water, I built a small fishpond edged with stones and ornamented with low plants. The hanging bronze lantern is a Momoyama-style piece.

The small lawn garden (Fig. 133) in front of the reception room is planted with Japanese stewartia and cryptomeria cedars. The azaleas along the top of the stones obstruct the view from the outside. Fig. 134 shows the pond and waterfall as seen from the living room. As is plain from the detail of the waterfall stone arrangement in Fig. 135, to achieve the effect required, the stones must lean as they do here, but for stability they must also have level tops and maintain balance in all directions. Notice that the top of the central stone, over which the water trickles, is straight. In addition, the stones on its right and left have horizontal tops, and the chipped surfaces of the wave-dividing stone below form horizontal step-like planes. Although lava stones rarely have many flat surfaces, in this case I was fortunate; consequently, maintaining the mood of the group, even though much of the stones' grain is slanted, was not as difficult as it might have been. The grain of the stone in the background slants to the right but is balanced by the grain of the smaller stone below, which by slanting to the left preserves the harmony of the group. The policy of balancing the forces—the grains—of all stones holds true in ordinary stone groups where smaller individual stones are positioned to suggest larger ones. Each must balance and be balanced by the others. The tree leaning into the waterfall from the left side is a camellia; other shrubs around the fall include black pine, maples, and oak. The long vines and colorful flowers of the wisteria on the right will complement the bright reds and golds of the carp. Water from the waterfall flows around the wave-dividing stone below and into the pond. This wave-divider, an important element in waterfall composition, is sometimes a group of two, three,

137. Stone group and raked gravel.

or five small stones. When the quantity of water flowing by it is great, a lovely white spray results. The view in Fig. 136 of the left side of the waterfall shows the thick planting, which, though not as luxuriant as it will later become, helps soften the total effect.

The sand and stone groups on the east side of the house (Fig. 137) consist of only paleozoic-strata crystaline pieces. By first setting the standing and leaning stones and then adding another leaning stone directed to the left and positioned beside the standing stone so as to counterbalance the first leaning stone and, finally, by adding a flat stone near the house, I was able to insure balance in the composition. Using a few flat-topped stones always contributes greatly to the stability of the group. Since this part of the garden enjoys a certain amount of sunlight, I planted grass and dotted azaleas and rushes here and there. Pouring concrete before spreading the white sand prevents unsightly mixing of sand and soil, and bringing the grass to the edge of the sand areas eliminates the need for small border stones. The traditional clay and tile wall, well suited to this kind of garden, will preserve the integrity of the mood even should tall buildings block the views of the neighboring trees. The small Japanese-style building on the left is a study and recreation room.

Fig. 138 shows the gravel plot next to the house and the stepping stones leading across the grass to the back gate in the southeast corner of the site.

Azaleas are planted along the top and among the stones of the rubble work fence. The cryptomeria and Japanese stewartia, visible in the mid-ground, are in the waterfall section of the garden. Farther to the right is the back entrance, and in the left foreground is the gate to the carport.

In contrast to the rough, severe stones designed for this house I should like to illustrate a gentler, rounded waterfall that I designed, in 1938, for the home of Mr. Sayuri Shibata, of Bay Bridge, Mt. Eden, California (Fig. 140).

138. Stepping stones leading to the back entrance.

139. Outside of the rubble work wall.
140. A restrained stone waterfall.

A Garden in the Shape of a Stream

The owner, a specialist in Noh-drama music, expressed the wish that the garden (Fig. 141) be in the shape of a stream, and since he is deeply imbued in traditional Japanese culture, the entire plan is purely Japanese in mood. The site, facing a public road on the southeast, though small, is well lighted and ventilated. The reception room, on the right in Fig. 142, is the only Western-style room in the house. The bamboo fence section and the double-tiered (Saimyo-ji style) bamboo gate divide the front garden from the inner garden. To the right of the gate is a pruned black Chinese pine. Views through open-work fences and gates are one of the most interesting aspects of traditional Japanese gardens. In Fig. 143, the same view with the gate open, the stepping stones, the intermediate pond, and the stream-shaped sand and stone group in the distance are visible. Contrary to the general practice of using a stream to feed a pond, this garden directs the overflow from the pond into the stream in much the same way as Lake Chuzen-ji, at Nikko, overflows to become the famous Kegon Falls and the Daiya River.

Instead of spreading white gravel loosely in the stream-shaped arrangement, as is the usual practice, I set a mixture of black, white, and blue gravel in concrete (Fig. 144). From the living room, the small natural stones on the far bank of the imitation stream are visible, whereas from the garden one sees the straight lines of the concrete and stone paved block in front of the house.

The fairly thick tree trunk on the left is that of a white plum which, when in bloom, contrasts nicely with the pink plum on the opposite side. In the upper center stands a *Ternstroemia japonica* with a gold-leaf plant and camellias below it. Around the stones on the right are planted such low shrubs as *Pieris japonica* and quince. By walking on the stepping stones at the end of the strip of pavement and crossing the stream arrangement one can proceed to the Domyo-ji-style stone lantern on the right of the plum tree. In the lower reaches of the stream (Fig. 145), though no water is actually present, the placement of the small stones, as if headed into a current, suggests flowing water. For more about directing stones so that they seem to exert force in certain directions, see Figs. 7 through 10.

The large tree in the center is a maple, and the slanting one on the left is a

141. Plan of the garden at the K residence.

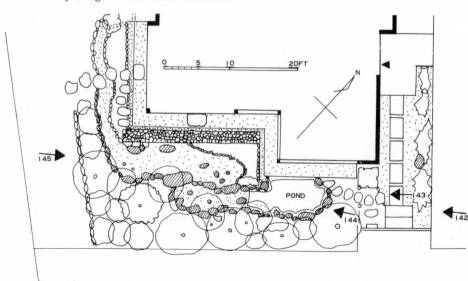

142. *Fence and gate.*   143. *View of the garden through the open gate.*

144. *Inner section of the garden seen from the gate.*
145. *View of the entrance from the inner section of the garden.*

pink plum. The pruned tree beyond it is a boxwood, and the evergreen in the background is a *Quercus myrsinaefolia*. *Rhododendra lateritium* conceal the roots of the pink plum.

Sometimes water flows through the stream bed, but that is not the point. In Japanese gardens interest centers on creating an effect, more than on literal interpretations; consequently, the stone banks, gravel bed, and the sweet flags planted here and there adequately evoke a waterside mood. The most important element, however, is the setting of the small stones in the stream bed: the heavily grained rock in the lower right corner seems to head into the stream; the flat top and scooped-out bottom of the stone farther to the left center and the one above it suggest movement. Embankment pilings sunk at random or overturned gabions are sometimes used in gardens to suggest the mood of the water's edge.

7. Front Gardens

In contrast to the Japanese system of enclosing all gardens with walls and fences, Americans create beautiful urban vistas by opening long connecting stretches of lawn from house to house. Though the resulting harmonious unity pleases, it is also a good idea to incorporate variety within that harmony to individualize each house. Being able to identify a home by its front garden, instead of by its number alone, provides interest similar to that exhibited in the small differences in cut and ornament of carefully tailor-made clothes. Variety of this kind plays a· large role in beautifying towns, particularly suburban areas where houses enjoy more spacious settings.

A Large Stone Group of Competing Forces

When the vast Japanese-style garden belonging to the Sumitomo family was destroyed to build this apartment building on the old site, I selected these two stones (Fig. 146) for use in the front garden of the new building.

Like the ferocious guardian statues at the gates to Buddhist temples, one with

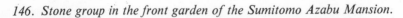

146. Stone group in the front garden of the Sumitomo Azabu Mansion.

147. Stone group entitled "Competition."

mouth gaping open and one with mouth clamped shut, these two stones seem to balance each other perfectly. The first roars and rages like a furious lion, while the other, lying slyly in wait like a crocodile, eyes the lion's tail and waits for a chance to snap. So well matched are the forces of the two, neither winning and neither losing, that I have called the group "Competition." Fig. 146 shows the group as it stands inside the entrance to the apartment building lot; Fig. 147 is a diagramatic representation of the stones' forces. The group symbolizes the countless struggles being waged in everything from the cosmos to man and the smallest atoms to preserve all-important balance.

I set the stones in vivid relief against a background of pruned boxwoods, spread the ground around them with white gravel, and dotted Dutch rushes here and there.

Front Garden with Parking Space

The combination of a Western-style house with Chinese black pines in the front garden (Fig. 148) of a house discussed earlier (see Figs. 72 and 73) creates a distinctive loveliness. To compensate for the height differential between the road and the house—three feet from gate to entrance and an additional three feet from the entrance to the level of the inner garden—I used Japanese-style rubble work planted with *Rhododendron lateritium*, Japanese silver leaf (*Ligularia tussilaginea*), and ferns and with *Rhododendron Azalea* along the tops of the stones. Between the fence post and the large stone to the left of it, a natural-

148. *View of the rubble-work wall from the right side of the front garden.*

(*left below*)
149. *Area in front of the entranceway.*
(*right below*)
150. *Parking lot in front of the entrance.*

stone staircase leads to the inner garden. Fig. 149 is a view from the rubble work across the parking area to the opposite side of the garden, where a *taiko*-style stone lantern stands among cryptomeria cedars and some large miscanthus that were a part of a previous garden on the same site. Occasional large stones and a row of smaller individually set, flat-topped stones separate the planting from the parking area. The view from the top of the rubble work (Fig. 150) shows the undulations in the lawn and the round-pruned *Rhododendron indicum*. Rubble work is used again to make up for the height difference between the lawn and the parking area on the far left.

Front Entrance with a Natural-style Retaining Wall

Cutting away the slope to make a driveway exposed a large section of steep cliff. To combine the utility of a retaining wall with the beauty of natural stone, I set rocks in concrete against the cliff as if a landslide had exposed them (Fig. 151). Among the stones are planted bamboo grass and ferns. Indigenous black pines, chestunuts, zelkova, *Eurya japonica*, and *Quercus serrata* cover the slope above the stone wall. Only the bamboo (*Phyllostachys pubescens*) on the far right was planted during garden design. I set fairly conspicuous rocks on either side of the entranceway and planted bamboo (*Chimonobambusa marmorea*) on the left. The plain wooden gate harmonizes with the rustic mood of the setting, and the paving sones set in concrete on the slope of the drive both contribute to the atmosphere and provide a slipfree road for vehicles. The highway in the foreground slopes gently downward to the left.

151. Road and gate at the base of the hill.

152. A large stone and birches outside of the inner gate.

Birches and a Stone against a Stone Wall

Cryptomeria cedars surround most of this garden—the same one shown in plan form in Fig. 23 and in photographs in Figs. 74–79. To vary the mood I paved the wall with brown slabs of natural stones, set a large blue stone at its base, and let the white lines of the birch trunks highlight the composition like bright strokes in relief. *Pieris japonica* is planted around the stones, and moss covers the ground. Gravel on a fine wire mesh conceals a manhole. The low shrubs in front of the small wall are boxwoods.

Small Plants and Stones

The narrow planted area between the house and the parking space (Fig. 153) contains a large, low stone set in grass with black pine, *Rhododendron indicum*, *Rhododendron lateritium*, and winter camellias dotted from place to place. I avoided the feeling of a grove in front of the house (Fig. 154), because the garden is surrounded by a fine stand of trees.

153. View of the entrance from within the inner gate.

154. Plants beside the entrance seen from the area in front of the garage.

8. Gardens for the Backs of Houses

Traditional Japanese architecture, in which large sliding panels connect rooms with the garden, usually provides an inner garden—*oku-niwa*—to be viewed from the reception room or guest room. When the Japanese first imported Western architectural styles, after the beginning of the Meiji period, they used the small windows common to houses in Europe and America; but later, finding them unsuited to the heat and humidity of their climate, they returned to the large sliding panel and continued the custom of the inner garden. The area corresponding to the Western backyard in Japanese homes is usually a workaday place for storage and clothes drying facilities, although lately, people have begun dressing them up with flowers and plants. The gardens I will mention in the next few pages are of that kind. Should such a back garden connect with the house by means of a terrace where people sit and enjoy the view, however, it would functionally resemble the traditional *oku-niwa*.

The Comma Garden

I designed this garden in Fulton, San Francisco, in 1967, for the home of an American of Japanese descent. Chosei Shinoda, a Japanese gardener residing in Berkeley, executed my plans.

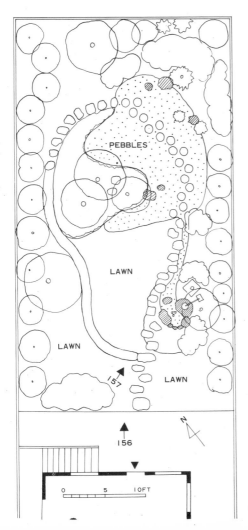

155. *Plan of the Comma Garden.*
156. *The Comma Garden.*

157. *Vicinity of the ritual water basin.*

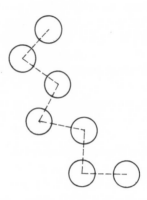

158. *Staggered stone placement.*

The comma—or *tomoe*—having nothing to do with punctuation, is a symbolic figure frequently used in the Orient. An ancestor of the owner of this house, a certain Hon-ami Koetsu, who lived in the late Momoyama and early Edo periods and was a man versed in many arts as well as a connoisseur of fine swords, is said to have designed a garden for a temple, the Honpo-ji, in Kyoto, which he called the garden of three commas (*Mitsu domoe no niwa*). With my client's consent, I used a similar idea for the raised planted areas and raked gravel, which forms a comma shape. Fig. 156 shows the completed central section, and Fig. 157 the area near the ritual water basin on the right.

I set one large and one small granite stone purchased in America in the far section of the garden, arranged another one slightly lower than the larger of the two former stones on the right, and let a flat-topped stone thrust peninsula-like into the gravel. Using as few other stones as possible, I brought the lawn covering directly to the edge of the gravel section.

The round stepping stones in the gravel are old millstones used for grinding beans and wheat. The owner bought several of them in Japan for an earlier garden. I have arranged them in a staggered fashion conforming to the stride of normal walking (Fig. 158). Stones of a perfectly round shape are well suited to a garden that adopts a particular form—in this case the comma—as its basis. The straight gravel line in the lower right of the picture is both a drainage trough for the ritual water basin and the dividing line between the moss and *Arenaria* sandwort used in place of grass. The American white gravel closely resembles Japanese Sakuragawa gravel. Clearly the United States has the materials to make raked-gravel gardens.

9. Gardens Close to Houses

Although, when small Japanese garden spots are combined with other garden elements or in very small exclusively Japanese gardens, a ritual water basin and stone lantern or some bamboo with gravel spread under it are the safest way to avoid difficulties, in the next case, where a Japanese element is incorporated in a predominantly Western garden, large stones do not seem oppressive because lawn and a stand of trees spread wide beyond them.

Fig. 66, another example of Japanese gardening elements used close to the house, shows my way of setting low stones under a group of deciduous trees.

A Stone Group Entitled "Waves Striking the Stones"

Noh actors symbolize the force of a downward strike by quickly raising the arm and gently bringing it down. Though this is in fact contrary to the action of striking, it is an effective symbol. Following a similar precept of mystic understatement, Japanese gardens symbolize the force of waves by placing stones to suggest a tremendous resistance to flowing waters. Both methods resemble symbolizing the right swing of a pendulum by means of drawing the pendulum to the left, except that the actual force is latent in the leftward pull, whereas in Noh and in the stone placement only the possibility of force is represented.

Both the restrained shapes and subtle grains of the large stones, seen from various angles in Figs. 159–163, contribute to a successful evocation of the feeling of resistance to strong currents and waves even though there is no water present. For this reason I have called the group "Waves Striking Stones." The pattern raked into the gravel around them further suggests water.

159. *Terrace and stone group.*
160. *View from the left of the living room.*

161. Stone garden and the reception room.
162. Entrance to the stone garden.

Fig. 159 shows the balance achieved by directing the force of the right stone to the left and of the left stone to the right. The border between the gravel and lawn sections is marked by a group of *Rhododendron lateritium* (Fig. 160); this is the only place where the two elements of the garden seem to join. I feel that it is good to make clear distinctions among garden elements of decidedly different characteristics, just as dramas require costume and scene changes. Had I wanted to use these stones as part of the whole garden, I would have set them back in the low pruned shrubbery in the background, but I decided to treat them as a picture set in the spacious lawn area instead.

Fig. 161 shows the relationships between the undulating lines of the stones and the living room in the background.

90   JAPANESE GARDEN ELEMENTS IN VARIOUS SETTINGS

*163. View of the stone group
and the raked gravel.*

The low flat stone in the middle of Fig. 162, a place to stand when stepping from the living room into the garden, provides a note of placidity in contrast to the vigorous activity of the larger stones. Fig. 163 reveals the parallel relationship between the raked gravel pattern and the edge of the terrace.

Garden in Front of a Semi-basement

The garden in Fig. 164 is part of the one shown in plan form in Fig. 23. It is a small area lower than the spacious main garden, but higher than the level of the semi-basement. In it I have planted bamboo (*Phyllostachys heterocycla*) and rhododendron and have spread white gravel. The entrance to the semi-basement is on the right of the rhododendron.

To soften the feeling of the mortar retaining wall, I have planted a cover of phlox (*Phlox subulata*).

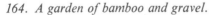

164. A garden of bamboo and gravel.

165. A garden with ritual water basin and bamboo.

Bamboo Grove with a Ritual Water Basin

I have already mentioned the advantage of using a simple water basin or stone lantern in cramped areas near the house. This particular example, though part of a garden for a teahouse attached to the main building, further illustrates my point. The outer *roji* extends to the end of the paved stone section (Fig. 165), and the grove on the left is the *Phyllostachys heterocycla* (var. *pubescens*) variety of bamboo.

10. Gardens on Concrete

Although a concrete surface strong enough to bear the load of about one foot of topsoil permits gardening identical in most respects with that carried out on the surface of the ground, sometimes only slight differences in height between the concrete and the floor level of the adjoining building cause serious drainage problems, or the presence of basement rooms or underground parking lots beneath the site of the planned garden makes drainage all but impossible. In such cases last resorts might include using potted plants or building a large box-like affair to hold the garden, but an easier way out of the dilemma is to construct a Japanese-style stone and gravel garden. Select stones with flat bottoms that do not require deep setting for stability, and although the thickness of the gravel layer is arbitrary, two or three inches are enough to create a good effect.

Flood Tide in the Harbor

Formerly the gardens of the mansion of a daimyo, the site was rich in fine stones, but most of them were of shapes difficult to set without burying to some depth. Since there are basement rooms under the concrete on which I had to construct the garden, I carefully mounded the gravel around the bases of the stones to conceal their pointed bottoms and thus created the mood of flood tide in a harbor dotted with islands.

Blocked from the sun on the east, west, and south, the garden will not support grass, and since the level of the concrete is nearly the same as that of the building floor it was impossible to add sufficient soil to allow the planting of trees.

Furthermore, the presence of basement rooms beneath the garden limited the placement of the large stones, which must, for safety, be set directly over the structural beams.

In all stone groups the sizes, forms, and grains of the individual components must balance to produce a finished work of art. In this instance, main stone A, and smaller stones B and C form a sub-group within the whole, (force directed to the left) and stone D, though apparently only half as large as A, effectively balances it by opposing its flow of force. Stone E, a flat stone with force balanced among all directions, is placid in itself, but it enlivens the total group to such an extent that without it the arrangement would be lifeless. Developing an eye for the importance of stones of this kind takes a little experience. Although, when the garden was first constructed, gravel completely concealed the base of stone E, it has somehow slipped away revealing an indentation at the bottom.

Stone C could be directed toward or away from the main stone. My original intention was to turn it in the direction of A, but I later discovered its additional natural tendency to its present placement. At any rate, it is so overwhelmed by the size of the larger members of the group that its influence is slight. The view from the entrance in Fig. 167 shows the mounding of the gravel around stones A, B, and C, that produces the mood of flood tide. The balancing role of the stone on the left and the enlivening and stabilizing effect of the flat stone, set on a diagonal with the outline of the garden, are also clear from this picture.

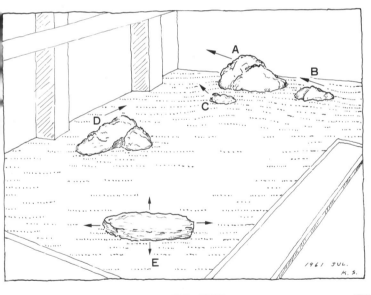

166. *Diagram of the forces of the stones in the inner garden of the Mitsui Life Insurance Home Office.*
167. *View from the entrance.*

168. *View from a position slightly farther right than that in Fig. 167.*

169. *View from the front of the building.*

170. *View from indoors.*

171. *The principle stone seen from indoors.*

Fig. 168 shows the *Gardenia jasminoides* planted between the garden edge stones and the paved walk. The limited amount of light that reaches the area will allow such plants as this and boxwood; azaleas, too, would live, but they would probably not bloom well. From a vantage point farther to the right (Fig. 169) stones D and E seem aligned. Although in most cases lining stones up this way is to be avoided, it is permissible if not apparent from primary vantage points. Views from the interior (Figs. 170 and 171, a little farther to the left) clearly reveal the variant force movements in small stone C; they also show how some of the gravel has slipped from the main stone.

The white wall at the inner edge of the garden develops a sense of boundless space which binds the garden elements together. The image of flood tide in a harbor would suffer severely if columns and glass surfaces took the place of that plain wall.

The Depths of a Canyon

The mood keynote of the garden, derived from the feeling of the tall enclosing building walls, the black boulders, and the blue-black gravel, is expressed in a poem:

> In the depths of the canyon, the muted voice of a great bird.

As was the case in the preceding garden, basement rooms beneath and a lack of level differentiation between the garden and the floors of the interior lead me to use stones and gravel instead of plants.

Stone A suggests the mystic qualities of canyons, and stone E is topped with living *Eurya japonica* as are many stones in remote bogs and hollows. A is large enough to balance all the other stones.

Stones A and E direct their forces straight up, B and D to the left, F and G to the right, and C, H, and I, flat stones, in an equal distribution in all directions. These last are, consequently, placid stones relating to all the others in the group. Because their force goes straight up instead of inclining in any single direction. A and E also belong to the placid stone category. By reacting, stones F and G and B and D provide movement, whereas A provides total unity.

172. *Diagram of the stone forces in the inner garden at the Japan Broadcasting Corporation's broadcasting center.*

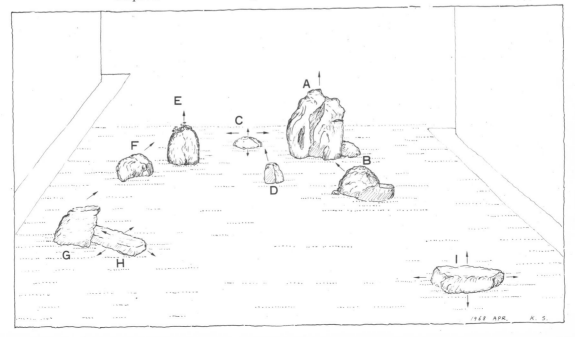

1968 APR.   K. S.

173. Distant view of the inner garden.
174. View of the opposite side of the same
     stone group.

175. View from a spot corresponding to
     the right corner of Fig. 172.
176. View of the opposite side.

Fig. 173 is a distant view of the stone group nestling at the bottom of the well created by the building and suggestive of a deep ravine. The main stone is the large one on the left. Fig. 174 is a closer view from the building side of the garden, that is, from the left corner of the stone-placement chart. Fig. 175 shows a view from the right corner of the stone placement chart, and therefore reveals the diagonal right side of the main stone. The low stone to the right of the main stone provides stability which might be lost because the large stone, from this vantage point, seem to incline backward.

A view from the opposite side, Fig. 176 shows how the sunlight illuminates the back of the main stone, which now seems to lean in a direction opposite to that suggested by the view in Fig. 175. The best side of the stone, that midway between those shown in Figs. 174 and 175, is directed toward the most important room facing the garden.

11. Courtyard Gardens

Although, by definition a garden enclosed by a building, the term courtyard garden includes the preceding two examples, I set them apart because they are limited by the concrete base on which they were constructed. The following courtyard garden employs soil and plants.

In many instances, in the United States and Europe, bright sunlight makes open gardens desirable; and even in shadier places, there are grasses that, unlike Japanese grasses, grow, if not as luxuriantly, in shade as well as in the sunlight. A person possessed of great horticultural talent could, if he chose, convert the courtyard spaces in his buildings into tropical jungles filled with exotic plants, but he might also decide in favor of the more serenely subtle beauty of Japanese gardens specially well suited to semi-shaded areas.

Miscanthus and Miscellaneous Trees

Miscanthus and camellias conceal the drainpipe and block the view, but the controlling element in this courtyard is the grove-like mood produced by a number of trees, only the trunks of which, unfortunately, are visible in the pho-

177. Inner garden in front of the dressing room.

178. Right side of the same garden.

179. View of the dressing room veranda from the corridor.

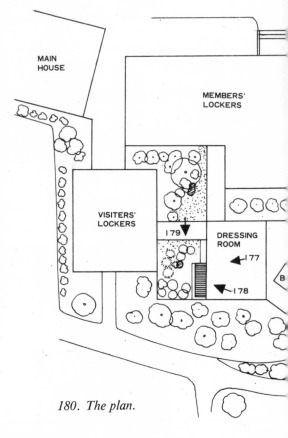

180. The plan.

tographs. Although oaks, weeping cherries, maples, or practically any tree of suitable size would have been suitable, I used eleven dogwoods that were already on the site. *Pieris japonica* surrounds the base of the single reddish flat stone in the center of Fig. 177. Grass is planted in the section containing the trees, and the rest of the ground is covered with gravel. Fig. 177 is the view from the dressing room, and Fig. 178 the one from outside left of that same room. The corridor visible through the trees leads from the bath to the locker rooms. Gravel spread at the edge of the veranda, in a trough outlined by a low concrete partition, provides rainwater drainage. The evergreen miscanthus, contrasting with the deciduous dogwoods, conceals the vertical drainpipe from the dressing room.

A second courtyard garden on the other side of the corridor is planted with large zelkova trees and camellias with *Pieris japonica, Illex serata*, and ferns under them.

In the view from the corridor toward the dressing room veranda, winter camellias block the openings in the lattice fence.

12. Gardens for Rooftops, Interiors, and Spaces under Floors

Similar to the gardens for concrete surfaces in that they are constructed on waterproof concrete, rooftop gardens are different because they usually enjoy abundant fresh air and sunlight.

In the cases of interior and under-floor gardens, however, the designer suddenly appreciates the wonder of the free, boundless sky because he can only lament its absence when his work must be done in dark areas. But there are two good points in totally enclosed gardens. One is the effectiveness of certain plants and stones and gravel in artificial and subdued lighting. The second is the elimination of distractions and the resulting increased possibility of appreciating garden elements to the fullest. Although grasses and plants will not last indoors, gravel and stone arrangements are frequently lovelier there than in the sunlight.

Gardens under floors, because a certain amount of digging is possible, are in some respects easier to construct than indoor gardens, but, ventilation is rarely good.

Sporting Seals

Though not a direct representation of seals, these small stones (Fig. 181) by contrasting movement, strengths and weaknesses, and postures evoke the kind of lively playfulness dear to those animals. The angular gravel is easy to rake into ornamental patterns. A small amount of moss and grasses at the stone bases freshens the composition with green.

Pines, some miscanthus, and cherry peep over the wall, which is only as high as a handrail. The flat paved terrace in the foreground—the inner section of the one shown in Figs. 107–110—is outfitted with Chinese-style benches and serves as an outdoor sitting room. A row of large stones in front of the glass doors facing the garden separates the gravel area from the immediate vicinity of the house.

N

20 30Ft

181. Second-floor stone and raked gravel garden at the K home.

Garden with a Flume

An interesting version of a teahouse, this purely Japanese room is on the third floor of a Western-style, reinforced concrete home. Because too many trees create a tremendous maintenance burden, I have used only azaleas and ferns around the stones. Water flows constantly through the bamboo pipe, into the *kakehi*-style flume, and from there to the stone basin below. The lantern, partly concealed in the shrubbery, is Momoyama style. Unfortunately, the hanging bamboo curtains obstruct the view of a nearby temple pagoda, which greatly dignifies the atmosphere of the tearoom and the garden.

182. The third-floor tea garden at the K home.

A Stone Group Representing Friendship

In the indoor pond of the house shown in plan form in Fig. 23, I set two stones, one black and covered with moss, to represent the feeling of friendship. Five-colored gravel (white, red, blue, black, gray), about one inch in diameter, covers the bottom of the shallow (about six inches) pond (Fig. 183).

183. Stone group in a small indoor pond.

Japanese-style Rooms and Gardens in a Reinforced-concrete, Western-style Building

Striving for privacy, the architects, Yasura Yamamura and Morio Sato, devised a Western-style, concrete exterior for the restaurant Oshimizu, but employed Japanese rooms—except for the large banquet hall—on the second and third floors. Divided into those facing north and those facing south, these rooms have a narrow garden running along their outer sides, but a fence of rustic bamboo totally blocks all views of the outside world. After providing a soil layer six inches deep on top of the waterproof concrete of the terrace areas, they left the task of designing garden spaces up to me.

Without the bamboo fence, the south side would have had plenty of sunlight

184. Sketch of the Oshimizu Restaurant.   *185. Part of the front garden.*

and good ventilation; the north side too would have had plenty of fresh air. But the architects' insistence on private individual gardens, like those found in crowded Japanese residential areas—a maximum depth of eight feet, a minimum of two—forced me to use stones, lanterns, gravel, and water basins and plants that grow well in shade: bamboos, *Mahonia japonica*, and nandin, gold-leaf plant, fatsia, *Pieris japonica*, ferns, Dutch rushes, *Iris japonica*, mosses, Japanese snake's beard, and *Pachysandra terminalis*. Although changing the fence to suit each individual garden would improve the interior design, the resulting jumble would have been unthinkable from the standpoint of exterior uniformity; consequently, the same rustic bamboo fence appears in all of the gardens.

Containing entrance offices, kitchens, Japanese-style banquet hall, counters, and pantries on the first floor, the building employs central east-west corridors on the second and third floors and arranges the individual rooms to face either north or south of the corridor. (The resulting peripheral garden plan could be useful in designing apartment buildings.)

The floor plan of the south side of the third floor (Fig. 186) shows the long, six-foot-wide garden that serves three (on the right) of the four rooms on this side. Although the garden is, in fact, communal (Fig. 187), unless one steps into it, it seems to be divided into three small individual spaces.

In the plan of the whole three-room section, I more or less drew up the desirable forms and shapes for the stones, but since I used natural materials and was, therefore, unable to select strictly, the actual garden did not develop precisely in accordance with my original plans. This kind of natural variation is, however, a source of great interest. A certain amount of sunlight on the south side allowed the planting of bamboo (*Pseudosasa japonica*); I also put moss at the bases of the stone groups, arranged to seem carelessly strewn across a highland plain, and spread gravel close to the room (Fig. 188).

186. Plan of the south side of the third floor interior.

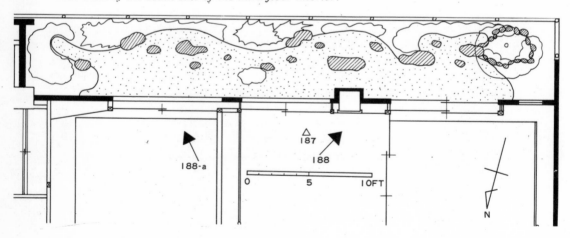

187. Sketch of the third-floor south garden.

188, 188-a. The right, and left sections of the same garden.

I omit illustrations and discussions of the remaining room on this side of the third floor because it is fundamentally similar to the one shown in Fig. 188.

Fig. 189, a plan of the north side of the third floor, shows the hall and the two private dining rooms; Fig. 190 is a sketch of the garden, and Fig. 191 a photograph of it. In this instance the bamboo stoop matches the mood developed by contrasting natural stones and gravel with a straight section of stone pavement.

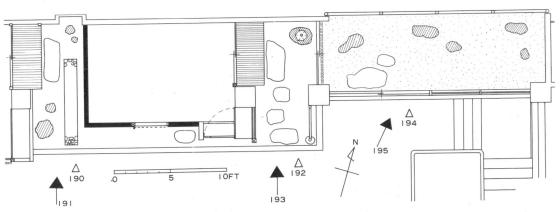

189. Plan of the third-floor north.

190, 191. Sketch and photograph of the third-floor north garden.

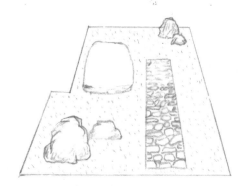

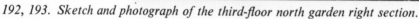

192, 193. Sketch and photograph of the third-floor north garden right section.

Stepping stones and gravel accented with a Sunshoan-style stone lantern at the innermost part of the north side of the third floor (Figs. 192, and 193), reveal the poignancy stones and gravel acquire when removed from natural settings and put indoors in a completely artificial environment. Sunshoan lanterns, set low like this one, normally light paths; this one, however, is purely ornamental.

The low stones in front of the third floor hall are easy to arrange, but they alone cannot carry the weight of the entire composition. They need the help of the standing stone on the left; nevertheless, it too must be assisted by a lower standing stone (right corner) to avoid a feeling of lonely instability. The ground is spread with two grades of gravel, but no plants are used, though English ivy or *Pachysandra terminalis* might have been attractive. Fig. 194 is a plan of the garden, and Fig. 195 a picture of it.

194. Sketch of the garden in front of the third-floor north hall.

195. *Third-floor north garden.*

196. *Plan of the second-floor south.*

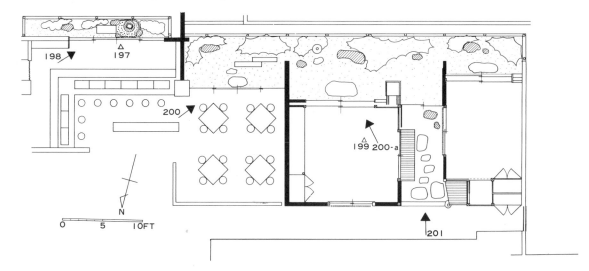

198.▼ 197 200▶ 199 200-a 201

N

0   5   10FT

Figs. 196, 197, and 198 are plan, diagram, and photograph of the south side of the second floor.

The extremely narrow (two feet) section of garden space behind the counter restricted the materials to a Fusen-shape water basin, accompanying stones, and a single stone slab, plus two grades of gravel. Some ferns would be pleasant planted along the edge of the fence. The plot is so small that photographing all of it is prohibitively awkward.

Fig. 199 is a sketch of the garden plot outside of a lounge area and two Japanese-style rooms. Although the garden is actually communal, partitions of bamboo and branches divide it into individual sections. The left corner of the garden appears in Fig. 200. Stepping stones and two staggered long rectangular stones are the primary elements of this section, and, though it is not shown in the photograph, I planted bamboo (*Semiarundinaria fastuosa*) in the left corner in a slightly mounded section of earth held in place by a few stones. Conventionally, rectangular stones are staggered so that their long sides overlap, but never so that a short side intersects a long one perpendicularly. The lower arrangement in the right of Fig. 199 is the ideal overlap for such stones, but when

197. *Diagram of the left side of the second-floor south garden.*

198. *Left section of the second-floor south garden.*

199. *Sketch of the garden in front of the lounge.*

*200, 200-a. Far left corner and
center of the right section
of the second-floor south
garden.*

*201. Inner garden on the
second-floor south.*

a slightly smaller overlap is required, the setting shown above it is suitable. A smaller overlap creates a feeling of instability.

The stepping stones and gravel (Fig. 201) are at the entrance from the second-floor central corridor to the two south Japanese-style rooms. Beyond the lattice in the background is the garden shown in sketch form in Fig. 199. The bright light flooding through the lattices sets a mood in which ornamental fussiness is out of place; consequently, I have used only moderately small stones.

The garden (two feet and five inches deep) in front of the left Japanese-style room on the second-floor north is so small that I omit a photograph of it. It contains only a single red stone with moss at its base and black Nachi stones on one side and white Nachi stones on the other. Similarly, the garden in front of the right room is too small to allow more than five small stones and some gravel and Dutch rushes.

The main point of interest in this area is the middle zone leading from the corridor to the two rooms (Fig. 204). Since these are teahouse-style spaces, I have planned this garden to resemble a *roji* and have included only stepping stones and gravel with a boulder-shaped basin and a flume for ornamental highlight. The water overflowing from the basin, courses into the gravel on the floor and passes out through a drain at the bottom of the iron-pot shaped basin in Fig. 205. The designers suggested this point of emphasis because the name of the restaurant, Oshimizu, means abundant, clear water. The stepping stones (an average diameter of one foot and five inches) are a little larger than the ordinary for tea gardens (diameter one foot); the added surface area makes walking easier for cutomers who become slightly tipsy at parties.

Located in front of the second-floor hall, the garden shown in the sketch in Fig. 206 and in photograph in Fig. 207 contains only a small stone group, some gravel, and a single nandin. The cutaway section of the top of the fence, while permitting a view of a nearby grove of trees, is sufficiently high to block the less pleasing view of a crowded residential area.

Finally, the large black pine in front of the building (Fig. 184), moved from another section of the same site, hides part of the too imposing exterior and mutes the total effect of the building.

202. Plan of the second-floor north garden.

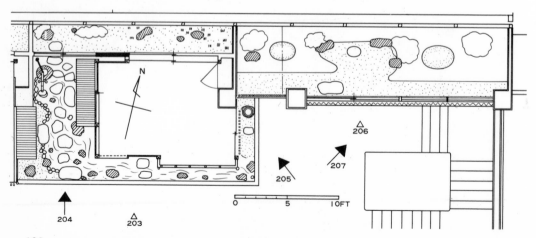

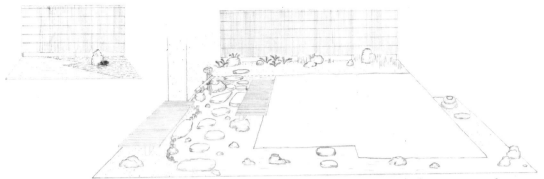

203. *Diagram of the garden in front of the two Japanese-style rooms on the second-floor north.*

204. Roji-*style garden on the second-floor north.*
205. *Iron-pot-shaped basin in the second-floor north* roji-*style garden.*

206. *Sketch of the garden in front of the second-floor hall.*
207. *Garden in front of the second-floor hall.*

Garden Beside a Sunken Parking Lot

This parking space under the elevated floor of the house has a maximum of about thirty minutes of sunlight each day, but that is enough to sustain the *Pieris japonica* and gold leaf plant that I have used to soften the rigidity of a predominantly stone decor. The main stone is balanced by an accompanying stone half its size, and both are set in white gravel: blue or blue-black gravels would produce too gloomy a mood. Had the retaining wall been clay, instead of flat masonry, it would have been possible to omit the plants; and in such a case, spatial balance would bé achieved by separating the stones more widely.

208. Small garden at the side of a basement garage.

13. Gardens for the Far North and for the Highlands

Although actual examples of Japanese gardens created in other lands tend to concentrate in regions between the fortieth and sixtieth parallels and at elevations of roughly six thousand feet, as long as the materials used are stone groups and gravels, no geographical limitations apply. Such gardens are as much at home in the frozen north as in the tropics, in deserts or on isolated, windswept islands.

Plants, on the other hand, present a number of problems. The silver firs in Fig. 209, transplanted from one of the northernmost of the Japanese islands, thrive in this small Tokyo garden of bamboo grasses, stone group, and a Shibo-butsu-style water basin. Usually, plants brought from extremely cold pace suffer no injury from transplantation to more moderate climates, though pines lose some of the handsome mosses and lichens that adorn their bark in colder zones. Most of the deciduous trees used in traditional Japanese gardens will stand cold; exceptions, however, are pomegranate, rose of Sharon, *Hibiscus mutabilis*, and *Albizza Julibrissin*. Birches will thrive only at elevations be-

209. *Garden consisting of a grove of silver firs.*

tween three and four thousand feet. The needle-bearing evergreens are hardy in cold weather: silver fir, white fir, *Toxus cuspidata, Picea jezoensis* (var. *hondoensis*), *Tsuga Sieboldii, Tsuga diversifolia, Pinus pentaphylla,* and *Pinus parviflora.* The broad leaf evergreens that will stand the cold are fewer, including only camellias, *Osmanthus ilicifolius,* and mountain laurels, but with these and the other trees mentioned above, creating any of the Japanese garden types is completely within the realm of possibility.

14. Gardens for Hot Climates, Deserts, and Seaside Regions

Most of the plants from the colder regions will thrive in warmer ones and if properly clipped and pruned will produce something like a true Japanese gardens. Furthermore, the special beauties of full-leafed, brightly colored tropical plants lend themselves to grove-and-spring-style gardens.

In desert zones, rock gardens with cactuses casually arranged suit the general tone of the setting, but by treating the stones and sands in a Japanese way and using the cactuses as plants to conceal stone bases, it is possible to introduce freshness into the desolation of wide stretches of barren land.

Providing your own windbreak of closely planted wind-resistant trees (black pine, *Juniperus chinensis, Juniperus rigida,* camellias, *Pittosporum tobira,* wild peach, spindle tree, boxwoods, *Euonymus japonica, Daphniphyllum Teijsmanni, Viburnum Awabuki,* and *Rhaphiolepis umbellata,* will enable you to plant tea gardens or lawns even where salt-laden sea winds blow strong. Although high bluffs close to turbulent seas present difficulties, stone and gravel groups with a mixture of *Juniperus rigida* and lawn generally solve most problems.

Usually undesirable because of the proximity of the sea, garden ponds may, however, be constructed in corners where the beach is not visible. In addition, fish in the pond add a note of movement. After all, nothing swimming in the sea, unless it is as big as a whale, will be visible from a seaside garden.

At the Hama and Shiba Detached Gardens in Tokyo the interest of the changing water lines of inlets captivates with a kind of loveliness that the beach itself cannot offer. Such inlets, however, are impossible to construct unless the main body of water from which they flow is calm, like Tokyo Bay, because violent waves cause obstructions at inlet openings.

15. Garden by the Beach

Although in tropical zones it is possible to use palm trees in seaside gardens, in temperate regions the following trees with good wind resistance are advisable: black pine, Chinese juniper (*Juniperus chinensis*), needle juniper (*Juniperus rigida*), creeping Japanese juniper (*Juniperus procumbens*). The following, though less hardy than the preceding, may also be used: Japanese coral tree (*Viburnum Awabuki*), Mateba oak (*Pasania edulis*), bayberry (or candleberry myrtle, *Myrica rubra*).

Lawn, which survives seaside condition, or stone groups are most suitable. Figs. 210 and 210-a show a villa near a famous pine grove and beach at Numazu, in Shizuoka Prefecture. To harmonize with its neighborhood, the garden employs largely lawn and black pines. To reduce wind damage and thereby to prevent the trees from falling in storms the pines have been pruned thoroughly.

The long stone retaining wall at the top of the slope on the edge of the lawn also serves as a bench. Beyond the wall are black pines with azaleas, Japanese eurya (*Eurya japonica*), weeping forsythia (*Forsythia suspensa*), cotton rose (*Hibiscus mutabilis*), and Japanese hydrangea (*Hydrangea macrophylla*). Such wild grasses as bush clover and Japanese pampas are planted beneath them.

210, 210-a. A garden by the beach.

III
Constructing a Japanese Garden

1. Apportionments and General Layout

Simultaneous with the planning of the building, discussions among the owner, the architect, and the landscape gardener must decide the placement of the entrance and garage, determining factors in the sizes of the front garden and driveway, and the plan arrangement of the living room, bedrooms, and children's rooms, which limit the amount of space available for back garden. This book deals only with the apportionment of Japanese garden elements within the areas so established.

Whether you use a blueprint for the garden or do not, you must always lay out a general plan on the surface of the ground itself; you must decide which sections will be lawn, where the pond will be, and where to set the main stones and plant the principle trees. Once this rough plan is completed, the minor garden elements will fall in place by themselves. When you do not have a specialist arrange a plan for you, draw your own preparatory one on paper before marking out general areas on the ground with a stick. Though a small plan helps establish perspective more efficiently, it is always best to set the main points of the design at the site before finalization. When you have a more or less firm idea of the layout on paper, return to the site, mark the individual areas on the ground, and drive stakes to represent the main trees, stones, and lanterns to determine whether the your ideas actually suit the nature and needs of the available ground. Do not begin construction until you have corrected all faulty points. Use graph paper for your plan, and transfer the resulting placements and measurements to the scale of the garden, or using the corner of an existing building as a center, mark off diagonals at right angles, measure them, and convert them into a scale for your paper plan.

Curved lines measured and drawn on the ground with a tape, though attractive when viewed close at hand, often appear fussy when seen from a distance; plan them with the full prospect in mind. Similarly, in both planning and executing a garden design, be aware of the influence of the angle of elevation in all views. Elevation can sometimes make shrubs seem too tall though they are intended to appear low.

In all cases, except those of simple, straight lines and circles, it is a good idea to use a stick about ten feet long to sketch garden areas on the ground because this lets you see what you are doing from a greater distance and helps you keep the larger picture in mind.

Although you intend two trees to be six feet apart, the trees delivered to you may have a foliage spread so much wider than your plan permits that alterations

114

become unavoidable. The architect, in dealing with unchanging, more or less standardized building materials, can be sure that the house he builds will be what he designed, but because natural trees and stones are unpredictable, the landscape gardener must often revise his original concept if he discovers that a tree of the shape he needs for the beauty of the garden is bigger than he had planned.

2. Planting

A. Transplanting Times

Most important in transplanting, retain as many of the root hairs as possible; without them, no matter how propitious the time, the plant will wither and die. Season, nevertheless, plays an important role in the growth of the plant after transplantation. In sub-tropical zones, almost all trees, evergreen or deciduous, can be transplanted from mid-autumn till the end of spring, If these times are inconvenient, trees may still be moved in rainy seasons. Humidity is important, for under arid conditions, even great quantities of water poured around the roots will not counteract rapid evaporation from leaf surfaces and the resulting withering of the plant. Evergreens may be moved from mid-spring till the end of the rainy season—or until severe heat and dryness begin—or from mid-autumn until the first frost. In humid regions, late spring and early fall are good seasons. Transplanting in winter does not harm the trees, but the difficulties of digging in frozen ground make the work impractical or even impossible in areas of heavy snowfall. Mountain highlands and other regions where mists are frequent permit successful transplants even in the summer.

Although it is common sense to transplant most deciduous trees after the leaves fall and before the new buds appear, plants that are especially susceptible to the cold should not be moved till the new buds are out: pomegranate, rose of Sharon, *Hibiscus mutabilis*, and *Xanthoxyum piperitum* DC are cases in point.

B. Tree Roots

Divided roughly into three categories—horizontal, downward slanting diagonal, and vertical—tree roots absorb water and nutrients from the soil; they also stabilize the upper part of the plant against winds and other outside forces. Although they all participate in these general functions, each type is specialized to a certain extent. Located in the rich loam layer of the soil and connected directly with the formative layer of the trunk, the horizontal roots are responsible for nutrient intake. Attached to the semi-core of the trunk, the diagonally placed roots absorb moisture from the water-rich layer of the soil; whereas the long, vertical roots, penetrating deep into the hard earth, are extensions of the core—the backbone—of the trunk and both absorb water and stabilize the entire tree. I might, therefore, compare the horizontal roots to the head of the nutrition department, the diagonal roots to the water chief, and the vertical roots to the sheriff of a small community. The laborers, who actually do the work of absorbing both moisture and food, are the root hairs. Passing from the root hairs, to the small, medium, and large roots, to the trunk, and from there to the

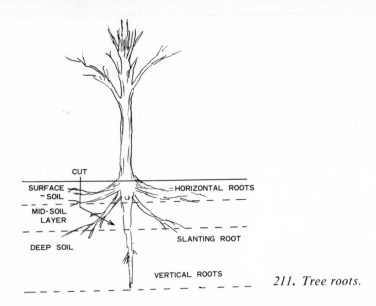

CUT

SURFACE – SOIL

HORIZONTAL ROOTS

MID-SOIL LAYER

DEEP SOIL

SLANTING ROOT

VERTICAL ROOTS

211. Tree roots.

large, medium, and small branches, and finally to the leaves, moisture and nutrients are converted into usable products and carried back along the same path to the lower reaches of the organism. In addition to manufacturing food, the leaves also evaporate excess moisture; that is, they are the plant's respiratory organs.

No matter how richly endowed with large roots, a plant devoid of root hairs cannot live: it is much like the proverbial chief with no Indians. Though the miracle of natural processes allows the plant to hurridly replace some lost root hairs, if all of them are cut off in transplantation, before they can be regenerated, the tree will wither. It is the gardener's duty, therefore, to devise a way to allow new root hairs to grow and thereby to prevent withering; the method we Japanese use is the *nemawashi*, explained in the following section. In this method, we take care to preserve the small roots, for it is from these that new root hairs develop. In contrast to a plant with plenty of small roots and root hairs, which will survive even in windy, arid conditions, one without these important organs will perish no matter how often it is watered. Root hairs work so miraculously that they seem to take in moisture from the very air. For best effect, fertilizers should be placed close to the small roots and root hairs.

Not all trees have the three classes of roots in the same proportions. For instance, the needle bearing evergreens and other high-rising trees, like the zelkova, develop pronounced vertical roots, whereas general evergreens, perenials, and deciduous trees whose trunks subdivide into numerous branches produce a preponderance of horizontal and diagonal roots. Trees growing on top of stones or those planted in areas where the ground water level is close to the surface develop no vertical roots but send their horizontal ones outward for great distances. The extra length results from these roots' having to perform the functions of the vertical and diagonal varieties. We call root-soil masses of comparative thinness *sarabachi* (plate-root mass) in Japanese because their roots and the soil attached to them assume the shallow rounded form of a dish. *Hachi* (phonetically *bachi* in this case) is the term applied to the roots and soil of a plant. In moving trees with long horizontal roots, it is imperative to dig wide to avoid damage. Once transplanted, trees from areas where the water level is high, must be watered frequently for a month or so until they become accustomed to their new environment.

C. Preparing, Raising, and Wrapping Roots and Pruning

Gardening conditions sometimes necessitate transplanting trees without making *nemawahi* preparations and with no more than a light pruning of the branches to open a view through them, but the percentage of successful transplantations in these cases is low. In other instances, particularly with deciduous trees that produce random buds when the large roots are cut, it is possible to prune extremely close, cut the main branches off, and move a tree with a ninety-nine-percent chance of success; but the plant is so unsightly that it is useless for immediate garden purposes. For these reasons, gardeners almost always employ the *nemawashi* system of preparing a tree for transplanting.

NEMAWASHI

Nemawashi, which should be performed on trees that have never been moved or on those that have been in their present location for roughly ten years, involves digging around the tree cutting the roots, lightly fertilizing, and returning the tree to its original position. The digging should be made in a circle the distance of one and one-half or two times the diameter of the trunk from its base Cut all the horizontal roots, except a few for support; then, digging from the periphery of the circle downward and toward a spot directly under

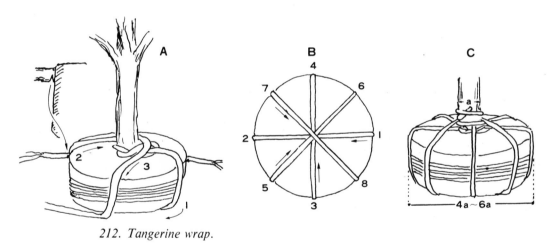

212. *Tangerine wrap.*

the trunk, cut all the the visible diagonal and vertical roots. After fertilizing lightly, return the soil.

Support against the wind must oe provided by leaving uncut one horizontal root in each of the four cardinal directions. They should, however, be triangularly nicked on the underside (Fig. 212-A, top left) to prevent their taking in water and thereby spoiling the effect of the *nemawashi*. By cutting all the other horizontal roots—even though the supports are left in place—it is possible to force the tree to compensate for necessary evaporation by using the nutrients stored in the trunk to rapidly develop many new roots. On the other hand, though nicked, the support roots protect even tall trees or those with wide spread boughs from falling in high winds.

A tree forced down by the wind, if it does not die, is forced to develop new roots just as is one that has undergone the *nemawashi* treatment.

One year after the *nemawashi* preparation has been carried out, the tree will be easy to transplant and will remain so until eight or ten years have passed, when it will become necessary to repeat the process. In performing *nemawashi* on old black or red pines, or on evergreen magnolia, which is slow to take root, cut the roots along half of the circle one year and the remainder the following year.

All trees sold for garden purposes in Japan must have undergone *nemawashi* preparation. A nursery that receives an order for a tree when it has no prepared one in stock, should, if conscientious, request the client to wait; the client would be foolish to insist on receiving an unprepared tree.

RAISING THE TREE

When raising a tree prepared for transplanting, it is imperative to dig in a circle wider than that used in the *nemawashi* process; usually a distance from the base of the trunk of four or six times the diameter of the trunk, at the point where it enters the ground. By breaking the roots closer to the trunk than they were cut in the *nemawashi*, too close digging will weaken the plant and greatly reduce its power of recovery, just as a human is weakened by a second surgical operation much more than by the first one. Be careful not to damage any of the new small roots stimulated by the *nemawashi* process.

TYING AND WRAPPING THE ROOTS

Although it is permissible to shake the soil from the roots of small deciduous trees being transplanted during winter and carry them to their new location, doing so increases the danger of root damage, particularly if the tree must remain exposed for some days. In this case it is wise to tie and wrap the roots just as must be done for all larger evergreens.

Being careful not to break or damage the roots, dig the tree up as you did in *nemawashi*, and beginning from the top, wrap a rope tightly around the mass of soil and roots in what is called a barrel wrap. In Fig. 213-A, the dotted lines represent the way the rope must look on the opposite side of the mass. I have used only one rope in the diagram to make the wrapping order clearer, but it is necessary to use more if the rope is weak. Leave an inch or two between coils if the soil is clayey, but wrap more closely when dealing with loose, sandy soil. As one person wraps the rope, another should pound it tight with a stake or an empty bottle. Tie it at the zone where horizontal roots stop and diagonal ones become predominant. Although we usually wrap from top to bottom, the reverse procedure serves as well.

213. Wrapping roots.

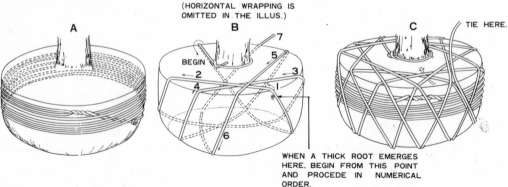

(HORIZONTAL WRAPPING IS OMITTED IN THE ILLUS.)

A   B   C   TIE HERE.

BEGIN

7
5
2   3
4 1
6

WHEN A THICK ROOT EMERGES HERE, BEGIN FROM THIS POINT AND PROCEDE IN NUMERICAL ORDER.

When the barrel wrap is completed, after attaching one end of the rope to the trunk, bring the other diagonally around the soil and roots in the manner shown in Fig. 213-B. Variations on this wrap—*agemaki*—include three-direction four-direction, and five-direction versions. All of these produce a crisscross mesh on the side, but they form an equilateral triangle, a square, or a regular pentagon when viewed from above. The ropes must cross the bottom of the root-soil mass horizontally in trees with no vertical roots or few diagonal ones. Fig. 213-B shows a four-directional *agemaki;* the completed wrap appears in Fig. 213-C. After determining, on the basis of the looseness or firmness of the soil, whether the wraps should be two or four inches apart, bring the cord around the root-soil mass as your assistant pounds it tight. Insert the free end under the wrapped rope, and tie it as the chart shows. Next lay the tree on its side, and using another rope, fill the openings in the bottom mesh so that the soil will not leak during transportation. In cases where vertical roots are totally absent, it is necessary to fill in the resulting cavity in the root-soil mass with earth.

For smaller trees that can be carried easily, use the simple tangerine wrap— so called because it suggests the sections of a peeled mandarine orange. After securing one end at the base of the trunk, wrap the rope across the top of the root-soil mass, down one side, straight across the bottom, and up the other side. After wrapping it around the trunk, cross it down and around so that it falls at right angles with the first. Taking care to keep the ropes equidistant from each other, continue around the mass. To protect the trunk in travel, wrap it with rope, leaving openings of about one inch, and cover it with a burlap bag, on top of which wrap another rope in coils spaced about three inches apart.

PRUNING

Since transplanting involves loss of a certain amount of water-absorbing roots, it is important to compensate by cutting away some of the branches bearing leaves, the organs of evaporation. While the tree is standing, examine it carefully

214. Pruning.

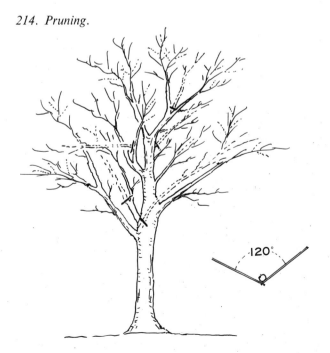

to decide which branches serve no beautifying purpose; when the tree is down, cut off these unnecessary parts, either at their bases or two or three inches from them.

In the latter case, you will have to remove the stub after the tree has been transplanted. The dotted lines in Fig. 214 indicate what I mean by unnecessary branches. Boldly eliminate unslightly bent branches, double ones, or those that result in excessively dense foliage. Avoid cutting a branch midway, for this produces an unnatural form; and cut to create a balanced amount of open space. If the foliage is too dense, even after the branches have been trimmed, prune away some of the leaves. To thin leaves of deciduous trees, which tend to wither when transplanted, draw the branches through your hands, starting at the base and working toward the tip. This will increase the chances of a successful transplant without damaging the buds.

D. Transporting

Each country employs its own methods of transporting all things, including trees for gardens. Although this makes exhaustive treatment here impossible, I would like to remark on two striking features of the way the Americans move trees. Because of the great care they take with plants, American gardeners dig up large root-soil masses making trees so heavy that movers can handle only one in the time in which Japanese gardeners would move five or more of similar size. In fact, the soil mass dug by American gardeners for a tree with a trunk diameter of four inches is as big as that for a one measuring one foot in Japan. The resulting increase in weight and decrease in the number that can be conveniently transported naturally raises the price of the transplanting procedure. In general, including large amounts of root soil and cutting practically no roots is an excellent idea, but since Japanese gardening demands precise placement of its elements, the tree must often be shifted about in its hole a great deal before the right posture is achieved. The resulting rough and tumble shakes enough soil out of the roots in large root-soil masses to be fatal to certain trees, like many of the pines, that are slow to develop the root-soil density necessary to their survival. Much the same thing happens with trees that are transported in wooden crates; they must, after all, be removed from the crates and planted; and this often deprives them of much important root soil. Of course, if the tree has been kept in a box or tub for some years, it has already produced a dense mass of fine roots accomodated to close quarters. Transplanting in that case presents no difficulty.

The interesting American use of empty cans for flowering shrubs and smaller trees could be valuable to Japanese gardeners. The cans themselves are trash and, therefore, do not affect the price of the plants, which, when planted in them, gradually develop dense, cylindrical root masses. Cutting the cans in half before planting and then tying them together reduces the amount of labor involved in transplanting and makes it possible to use the same cans over and over.

E. Planting

The hole for the tree must be about two feet wider than the root-soil mass and about five inches deeper than the mass is tall. The difference in the height of the mass and the depth of the hole should be made up by spreading rich loam in the bottom of the hole.

To stand the tree in place, attach three ropes as near the top as possible. One of these, a guide line, should be wrapped once around a nearby tree or stake and manned by one assistant to prevent the tree from falling. The other two, also wrapped once around trees or stakes, are used to raise the tree and should be manned by as many people as are needed. Being careful of the position and direction, raise the tree; correct any faults in placement.

After removing the burlap covering from the root-soil mass, cut away any roots that have been broken or skinned; then add good soil (rich loam or fertilized top soil).

There are two methods of packing the soil among the roots: with a stick and with water. Use the former for trees with good root-soil masses and the latter for those lacking soil. Although it is possible to use the water method with good root-soil masses, you must be careful not to shake out the soil already present. Adding water and soil together, when the hole is about seven-tenths filled, shake the tree to allow the muddy water to flow around the roots. Use only enough water to make the mud flow in and out of the roots. Correct the placement of the tree, and fill in the hole with soil.

By placement, in this instance, I mean standing a tree vertically if that is the

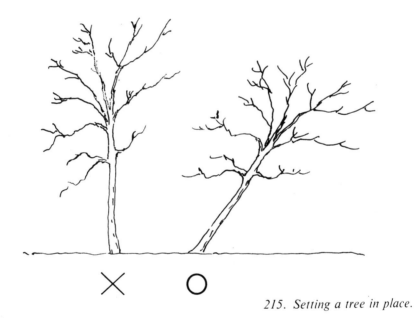

215. *Setting a tree in place.*

way it must stand, or inclining it, if it naturally leans. Vertical trees are easier to arrange, than inclined ones. In Fig. 215, I explain how a vertical position for a tree with sharply inclined limbs destroys the balance of the total form.

For trees with little soil around the roots, use a round stick, about two inches in diameter and about five feet long to push the soil in place gently. When the hole is roughly eight-tenths full, water well, and add the remaining soil. Usually, avoid shaking trees in this method, but when the hole is about three-tenths filled, it is permissible to rock the trunk lightly to work the soil among the bottom roots. On the other hand, move the root-soil mass, not the tree, if the diameter of the mass is as much as ten times larger than that of the trunk.

When the hole is filled, raise a four-inch mound of earth all around the base of the tree so that the top of the earth-soil mass become a hollow to hold rainwater. You might use a circular row of tiles or stones to achieve the same effect. Dig a four-inch-deep hole, circular or oval, on the upper side of trees planted on an incline to catch and make use of flowing surface water. These depressions are vital to the life of transplanted trees, but they must be visually inconspicuous.

Even small plants and grasses for the bases of trees and stones should be moved with the root-soil mass as much intact as possible, but *Rhododendron indicum* and *Enkianthus perulatus* seem to thrive on a change of soil around the roots, as long as they do not dry out from over exposure. Plants concealing the bottoms of stones and trees should be set neither too close nor too far away from the object they accompany. Furthermore, they will look more natural and attractive if planted one at a time instead of in clusters in large holes.

F. Props

Indispensable to newly transplanted trees, props are usually long poles tied to the high sections and to stakes sunk in the ground at the other end, where they themselves are buried to a depth of about one inch. For a tree twelve or thirteen feet tall use two poles set inconspicuously at 120-degree angles; for trees of more than twenty feet, use four poles set at ninety-degree angles (Fig. 214).

In addition to the plain pole, there are a number of other kinds of props, for instance a gate shaped prop and a triangular prop with a high cross arm. Both of these, usually buried about two feet in the ground, are made of logs that have either a 7 : 10 or 8 : 10 ratio to the diameter of the trunk of the tree supported. The T-shaped brace and the trapezoidal brace are used at the bottoms of trees planted to incline and are usually buried more than one and one-half feet in the ground. Examples of these are found in Figs. 31,40, and 100. Figs. 44, 47, and 109 show a horizontal brace consisting of a pole tied high between two trees to make use of the strengths of both for mutual support. Galvanized steel cables—one-eighth to one-quarter of an inch in diameter, depending on the size of the tree—can be strung in three directions and anchored to stakes in the ground to provide support in place of pole props. Though the cables will bury in the bark of the tree as it grows, they can be removed when the tree is firmly set.

G. Watering

Water tranplanted trees every evening for one month after moving; later, every seven days that it does not rain, and seven days after each rain, if dryness sets in again.

If winter is approaching, spread fallen leaves or humus over the roots of evergreens and other plants susceptible to cold to prevent freezing. If, however, summer is on the way, wrap the boughs and leaves with cardboard or heavy paper to prevent excess evaporation.

Finally, remember that newly transplanted trees fall victim to many harmful insect pests. In Japan, we use DDT and BHC against most bugs, carbon disulfide against borers, emulsified machine oil against scale insects, and Bordeaux mixture for diseases. Many good commercially prepared products are available in most countries.

3. Arranging and Constructing Stone Groups

Trees permit a certain amount of pruning and alteration to fit them into a pre-set garden design, but stones do not. Consequently, it is always a good idea to examine the stones available before designing the group. On the other hand, as he proceeds with his plans, a gardener frequently discovers exciting, heretofore unperceived beauties in certain stones that make changes in the design desirable. For this reason, the man who created the design should always supervise the construction. Convinced of the importance of this approach, I treat design and construction simultaneously in this section.

A. Setting One Stone

In transportation, a steel bar is used only on the back part of large stones, and the remainder is inclosed in a wooden frame. All parts that come in contact with cables or that might rub against other stones are protected with cloth or cardboard, because once a stone's fine patina or coating of moss—the product of years of development—has been damaged, it takes far too long for it to regain its lost beauty.

The buried portion of a stone is called the root, and the line at which it must be set to avoid looking top-heavy or unstable is its spread line. For instance, the stone in Fig. 216 would seem about to topple over if it were set so that any of the root—dotted lines—appeared above the ground line. Properly set, a stone should give no hint of much or how little of it remains underground. It is, however, permissible to disregard the root and the spread line when the desired effect is one of loosely scattered boulders.

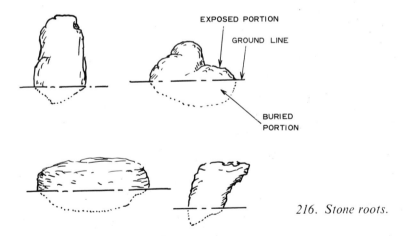

EXPOSED PORTION

GROUND LINE

BURIED PORTION

216. Stone roots.

The shape of the stone, and nothing else, determines how much of it should be buried and how much exposed. In Fig. 217, stones A and C, though at least half of each is buried, seem less stable than stones B and D, of which only about one-fifth is buried. The reason for the instability of the first two is their exposed root sections.

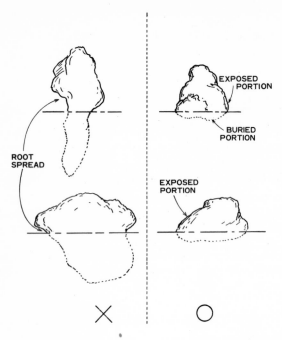

ROOT
SPREAD

EXPOSED
PORTION

BURIED
PORTION

EXPOSED
PORTION

X   O

217. Depths for burying lower parts of stones.

In order to determine not only the root, but also all of the other factors influencing stone placement you must be able to discern the front, back, top, and bottom of a stone. The front is the side that is most beautiful, that has the loveliest grain and color, the most elegance, and the fewest flaws. Its opposite side is, of course, the back. If two sides seem equal in beauty, have the owner of the garden decide which he prefers.

In any given setting, each stone has a definite top, a part that must be set upward. Determine which point should be uppermost, and set the stone accordingly. To violate this rule would be as senseless as having a human walk always on his hands. For instance, among the positions of the stones shown in A, B, C, D, and E, the top row of Fig. 218, C and E are clearly set with their tops up because all the other arrangements seem unstable. In E, the top of the stone and the spread line (dotted line) balance, and there is no mistaking the top of the stone in C. Since it is pointed, however, its ornamental value is inferior to that of the other stones.

The middle row of views of the same stone from the same surface turned in many directions indicates that D and E are tops, since they are flat and stable. Bear in mind, however, that no stone arrangement can use only flat-topped stones. It is in the combination of different stone forms that the difficulty of stone arrangements lies. If standing stone D were large it could be the protagonist of a group, whereas if it were small it would serve in front of main stone or in a pond. E would make a good wave-dividing stone in front of a waterfall, a stone for a set of rapids, one or two of stones in a pond arranged to suggest a pair of birds.

The grain of the stone influences its placement as much as the outline. For instance, A in the bottom row of stones in Fig. 218 is the same shape as A in the top row, but its grain indicates the setting. Although it is possible to set straight grains to run perpendicular to the ground, placed horizontaly they gain stability. The bottom row in Fig. 218 shows several horizontal and vertical

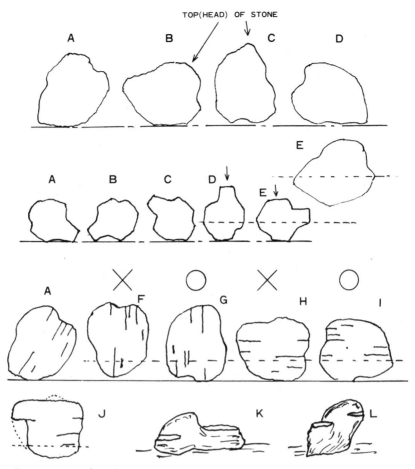

218. Stone tops and grains.

settings. Noting that G is more stable than F and I more than H, you will see immediately that the more widely spread section of the stone is generally best set at the bottom; however, a wide top projection more vividly expresses the distinctive role of the so-called peeping stones, (*nozoki-ishi*). For instance, to serve as a peeping stone, H should be cut out as shown in J. Furthermore, if the top in F were flat, that setting would effectively serve as a peeping stone representing a sheer cliff.

Stones with shelf-like sections (K and L) are rare in nature; set them so that the grain is horizontal and so that the shelf is parallel to the ground.

Finally, for review, I repeat: always set the head (top) of the stone upward for both standing or reclining stones; if the grain of the stone is inconspicuous, be sure that the top and the spread line balance. Arrange pronounced grains so that they are either perpendicular to or parallel with the ground; set shelf-stones so that the shelf-like section is parallel with the ground.

For perfect stability, set stones like that in Fig. 219 in position A, but if the demands of the group require movement instead of repose, set the stone so that the line of the top forms a small angle with the spread line: setting C, *not* setting B. We sometimes, though rarely, use stones with only a small part of the root buried or with the entire root exposed and with the upper section leaning on another stone to symbolize canyons or river beds.

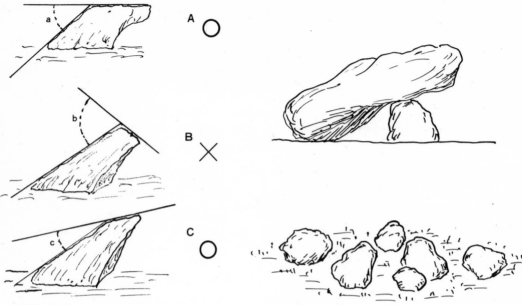

219. *Balance in a stone setting.*

220. *One stone leaning on another (above); free standing stones (below).*

Loosely scattered, unburied stones often serve a similar function, but they are usually too fussy for limited gardens. If, however, you feel you must use them in cramped spaces, select only small stones.

Every stone is shaped to relate in one direction or another to something in a garden—tree, body of water, or space—even when set without accompanying stones. In other words, each stone can be a group in itself. The gardener's duty is to discover the direction in which the stone most naturally relates and to set it to permit the formation of such a relationship. For example, the stone in Fig. 7 is set on the left to face to the right because its shape links it with the garden scene on that side. If it were set on the right of the garden, it would have its back to the area that should be its better half and would, therefore, seem to be winking coyly over its shoulder to its companion. The stone in Fig. 8, on the other hand, is set on the right side of the garden because its shape relates to the left.

Finally, in connection with actually setting the stone in place, I will make these few remarks. After having lowered the stone into the hole (Fig. 83), correct the direction and placement, and fill in the hole, using a small stick to pack the earth firmly till it reaches the level of the surrounding ground. Next tread the ground smooth, and with a soft brush clean away the mud and dirt clinging to the stone. Use water to wash away the fine particles of dirt, but never damage the irreplaceable patina and moss on a stone by scrubbing with a rough steel brush.

B. Grouping Several Stones

VISUAL AND SPATIAL CONSTRUCTION

Stone groups must dynamically prevent falling and crumbling while they aesthetically inspire the viewer with a sense of formal, rhythmical beauty, elegance, and spiritual repose. Even when the stones are set at considerable distances

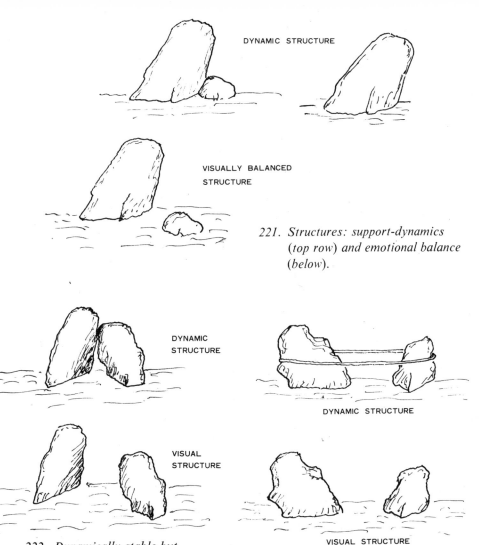

DYNAMIC STRUCTURE

VISUALLY BALANCED
STRUCTURE

*221. Structures: support-dynamics
(top row) and emotional balance
(below).*

DYNAMIC
STRUCTURE

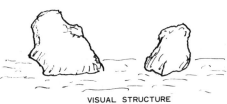

DYNAMIC STRUCTURE

VISUAL
STRUCTURE

VISUAL STRUCTURE

*222. Dynamically stable but
apparently unbalanced stones
and emotionally stable stones.*

*223. Visual balance can be achieved
without the use of a rope.*

apart, the group must cohere by means of the relationships among its individual elements. Though dynamically, physically, and structurally separated, the stones in a group must suggest stability as if they supported each other. Japanese gardens emphasize visual and spatial construction as much as actual physical structure, even in retaining walls where the actual dynamic role of the arrangement might otherwise tend to overshadow ornamental functions.

In the upper row of Fig. 221, the small stone in the group on the left dynamically supports the larger one, according to the principle of the fulcrum; but, though imbedded so deeply in the ground that physically it cannot fall, the single stone on the right seems about to topple over because it lacks the visual stability provided by the smaller stone. The effect of visual stability is still more vividly presented in the bottom set of stone in the same figure. Although the stones do not come into physical contact, their placement visually produces a stronger sense of stability than was possible in the upper group.

Fig. 222 offers a further example of the importance of visually stable constructions. The upper group seems firm and sure, as it should be since the two stones lean on each other for support. Viewed singly, the stones in the lower group appear in danger of falling, but taken as a unit, though separated by a considerable distance, they visually support each other.

Fig. 223 illustrates uniting two physically secure, but visually unstable, stones by means of the force of pull. The bottom group is set to manifest the same stability that the rope in the upper group provides.

VISUAL BALANCE

Balance of forms plays an important role in stone groups, as is clear from the placements of the stones in the top two rows of Fig. 224. In the upper row the majority of the weight of the group, by falling on the right side, destroys formal balance, which is restored, however, by placing the stones as they are in the middle row. It is vital to avoid setting three or more stones in a straight line because they will then seem unbalanced. Moving them as the dotted lines in the bottom row of Fig. 224 indicates solves the problem.

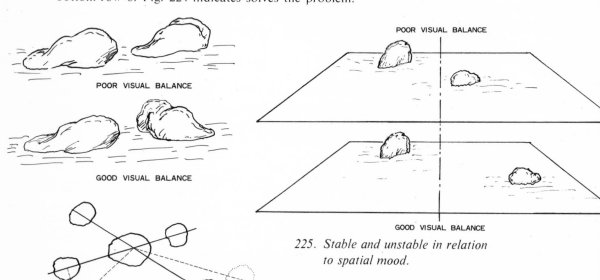

POOR VISUAL BALANCE

GOOD VISUAL BALANCE

POOR VISUAL BALANCE

GOOD VISUAL BALANCE

225. *Stable and unstable in relation to spatial mood.*

224. *Emotionally stable and unstable stone settings.*

In small gardens, like the courtyard illustrated in Fig. 225, where the central axis is easy to establish, balance must be maintained by using empty spaces as well as the stones themselves. The upper setting is one-sided, but separating the stones and opening a larger space in the middle of the garden puts the whole thing right again.

PRINCIPLE AND SUBORDINATE, PURSUER AND PURSUED

I have discussed such important elements in stone groups of more than two elements as stability and balance, but there are other relationships that bind a stone arrangement into a coherent whole; one such is the connection between principle and subordinate.

For instance, the large and small standing stones in the top of Fig. 226 bear the chief and subordinate relationship of parent and child or of employer and

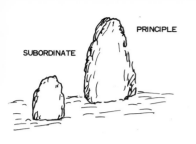

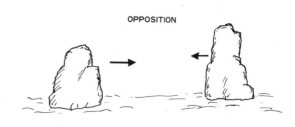

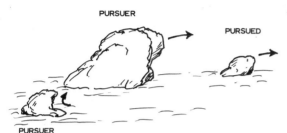

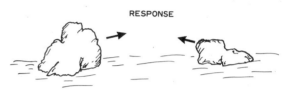

226. *The principle-and-subordinate or*
pursuer-and-pursued principle
applied to stones.

227. *Opposition and response.*

employee. By providing company to the large stone, the small one stabilizes the group and conversely receives strength and significance form its bigger partner. This relationship is a static one.

On the other hand, the stones in the lower group represent a dynamic version of a similar relationship. In this case, the large stone seems to chase the smaller one on the right, while the small one on the left tags along, as if at its mother's apron strings. This dynamic atmosphere of subordination and chase results from directing the symbolic forces of the stones in the directions shown by the arrows.

OPPOSITION AND RESPONSE

The symbolic forces of stones directed to create an emotional relationship (either opposition or response,) both enliven the stones themselves and create sparks of interest in the spaces around them. The two standing stones in Fig. 227 confront each other; they may seem to be scowling or laughingly inquiring of their healths; at any rate, an emotional relationship brings them to life, because their forces move in the directions of the arrows.

In contrast to the static opposition of the upper group, the two lower stones dynamically respond to each other as if whatever they have to say to each other must be uttered in a loud voice.

PROPORTIONS

The beauty of stone groups often depends on simple and pure proportions among elements. The large stone in Fig. 228 is twice as big as the one on the right, which is, in turn, twice as large as the smaller one on the left. Furthermore, the distance between the central stone and that on the right is twice the width of the smaller stone, and that between the left stone and the central one is the width of the smaller. Such simple proportions, similar to the modular systems used in traditional Japanese architecture, result in clarity and beauty. Of course, since the materials are natural stones, measurements are not as exact as those made by

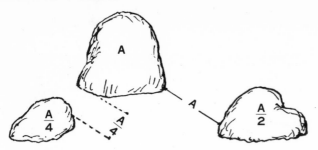

228. *Size and distance proportions in stone setting.*

a carpenter. In general, the smaller stones are used to determine distance: a large stone and a small stone will be separated a certain number of times the width of the smaller one.

RHYTHM

Whether in continuous lines along the banks of streams or in widely separated settings, rhythms of high and low, projection and recession advance to the climax of a stone arrangement, much as music approaches its peak moments through rhythmical variations. For example, at the side of calm, standing water, the stones must be placid; whereas they must be set to accent dynamically the movement of swift streams or rapids.

The illustrations in Figs. 229 to 234 show a rapidly flowing, abundantly watered stream where the stone setting took the form of a continuous bank of boulders and rocks. When the photographs were taken, the arrangement was still in progress, as is clear from its naked appearance and from the presence here and there of the gardeners' tools.

Beginning in the background, to the left of the large stone in Fig. 229, I first set a number of ordinary small stones then gradually added larger ones as I intensified the projections and recessions of the shoreline. The calm area of water, where the stones on the bottom are clearly visible, immediately precedes rapids, (Figs. 229 and 230). Although not shown in the photograph, wide areas of garden on either side of the stream balance the composition. After bringing in a load of sand and creating a bar below the rapids, I set the border stones to loom out over the water in some places and to lie close against it, their bases lapped by the waves, in others. In Fig. 231, the stones jut well into the stream at a point where one flat rock is placed in the middle of the water to permit passage across.

Just above the wave-dividing stone, churning the water of the rapid (Fig. 232), a large pitted rock resting on two other large stones spans the stream. Fig. 233 is a view of the lower reaches from the bridge-like stone in the preceding figure. The large stone in the water and the placid standing stones beside it reinforce the calm in this area where the flow slows down for a moment to become so deep that, though clear, the water hides the bottom of the stream. From this gentle mood the stream rushes to the waterfall (Fig. 234), the climax of the entire arrangement. In contrast to the virile, double-stage main fall, where the water froths white around the wave-dividing stones, a gentler, feminine fall adds a charmining, plaintive note to the left side of the scene. Both pour their waters into the same basin, set with a few large and small wave-dividing stones. The water flows from this high point of the stone group to a large pond.

Incidentally, trees and stones leaning toward the waterfall opening intensify the natural mood.

229. *The stone group, beginning at the inner left of the large stone,*
230. *Rises and falls,*
231. *Recedes and projects,*

232. *Seems to leap upward,*
233. *Opens views like this one from the leaning stone downward to the lower reaches of the stream, and*
234. *Finally approaches the climax of the entire arrangement.*

C. Moving Stones into Place

Adjacent stones are set in two fashions: standing against one another, or leaning on one another. In the former case, they may be set just as single stones, but in the latter, they require different treatment. Although the general rule is to set the support stone first and then lean the other on it, with very large leaning stones and small support stones, reverse the procedure: first set the large stone temporarily as desired, then raise it with a chain and block. Insert the support stone in the proper place, and lower the large stone. To prevent damage to the surface of the stone, it is imperative to insert pieces of wooden stake between it and the chains of the block and tackle and the cable surrounding the

235. *Temporary setting.*

236. *A wrecker used in setting stones.*

stone (Fig. 235). For extremely large stones, a wrecker crane is useful (Fig. 236), but no matter what equipment you employ, you will find that carefully attaching cables and wires so that the top of the stone is up and so that it is turned generally as you want the final setting will greatly lighten your labor. Because this is not easy, however, it is often necessary to attach the cables, lift the stone, lower it, and correct the cable placements several times before the stone is where it should be. The stone in Fig. 236 weighs over five tons; consequently, the wrecker is indispensable, but levers will suffice for stones weighing up to about 600 pounds.

Fig. 237 is a diagramatic representation of the way to attach lifting cables to a stone. Once the stone is in the correct head-up position, make a loop with one end of the cable at the upper surface of the stone, and bringing the other end through the loop, attach it to the block. Line A is clamped in place by the weight of the stone, which is supported by line B; and line C is held securely in place between line D and the bottom of the stone. It is necessary to pull A until the weight of the stone is supported by B as the tackle raises the block. Shackling A and B gives even greater safety: when dealing with stones of great size, always choose the safest method, even though it may require a little more time and effort. The W tie shown in the upper right corner of Fig. 237 is very safe.

Always following the principle of the lever and the arch, set vertical stones to that they seem to support each other.

A specialist will have a good idea of the placements and the settings of all the stones in a group before he starts work—I can, for instance, remember about twenty—but it is necessary to have a clear mental image of only the second stone before setting the first one.

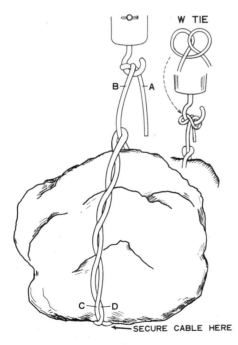

W TIE

B — A

C — D

←SECURE CABLE HERE

237. Support ties.

RUBBLE-WORK RETAINING WALLS

The retaining wall in Fig. 148, because it contains a number of large ornamental stones, is less a pure rubble-work wall than the one in Fig. 238, which is designed to give the feeling that rocks from above have tumbled down until they reached the condition shown in the diagram.

Although unnecessary for light walls of no more than two or three feet in height, heavier ones of five feet or more require the foundation pictured in Fig. 238: a layer of closely packed, rough gravel topped with five inches of concrete. Such a wall is safe from collapse, even should part of the foundation slip be-cause the stones mutually hold each other in place.

After the foundation is completed, begin the wall by setting the first row of stones: the root stones. Leaning backward to resist earth pressure, these stones, (1, 2, 3, and 4 in the diagram) must rest directly on the foundation because they bear the weight of the stones above them. They must be roughly triangular in shape to prevent the stones leaning against them from rolling over, as the arrow in the bottom row of Fig. 238 indicates. Furthermore, the sharpest angle of the triangle must receive the stone above; in the intermediate stones as well as in the root stones, the apex of the triangle should be set downward. Placing all the stones—including the small fill-in ones like C and D—so that their tops are level results in a more elegant wall. Ferns and small plants may be inserted in the cracks among the stones.

Not all of the stones above the root stones need touch the foundation, but at least those in the second row should do so. To increase the formal feeling of a wall, set the top stones in a straight line; on the other hand, for a natural, lighter mood, let some of them rise higher than others. Drainage demands that you either fill the area behind the stones with gravel and then return the natural soil or that you leave one-inch holes in the wall at intervals of five feet. When the stones are in place and the small ferns planted, brush them clean, and finally wash them with water.

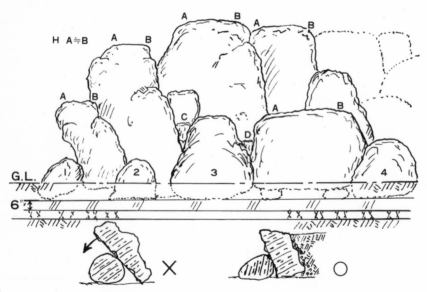

238. Rubble work walls.

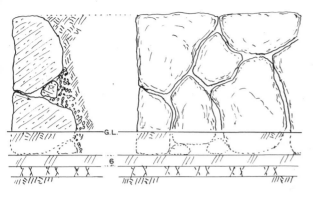

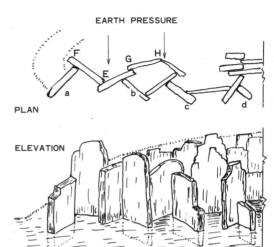

SCREEN-STYLE STONE GROURING

239. *Tortoise-shell-pattern masonry.*

240. *Stone slabs set to resemble a folding screen and stake settings.*

INFORMAL STAKE SETTING

ALTERNATING
STAKE SETTING

INFORMAL TORTOISE-SHELL PATTERN WALL

A brief explanation will suffice, since this kind of wall is already widely used in the West. In this informal version of a more rigid wall pattern, the first problem is to select from a large number of stones, the ones that will make a perfectly straight top line for the uppermost layer. All of the other stones need only be of shapes that permit setting their upper surfaces level. Lay a foundation (Fig. 239), and leaving about a foot between it and ground level—sufficient space to conceal irregularities in the bottom row—set the stones so that they are deeper than their exposed surfaces are wide. This is not always possible, however, with very large stones. They should taper toward the rear (see cross section) to prevent those set above from sliding forward. Fill the interstices between large stones with small ones. As in the preceding wall, fill the back with gravel and natural soil for drainage, plant azaleas or ferns among the stones, and clean them gently, but thoroughly, when the entire arrangement is finished.

STANDING-SCREEN STONE WALL

Mentioned in the *Sakutei-ki,* a famous Japanese gardening classic, a wall of thin, wide, flat stones set at angles similar to those of standing screens not only withstands considerable earth pressure and, therefore, serves as a retaining wall, it also creates a beautiful cliff effect. The upper part of Fig. 240 is a plan and the middle section a diagram of such a wall, in which only *a, b, c,* and *d* are set deeply in the earth; the others lean against them. Simply burying the root stones provides secure retaining power since the force acting on one stone (E) is balanced by two others (F and G). Two stone panels abut at point H. Do not continue such walls for more than two or three levels, because overextended they become fussy and lose some of their structural strength. More than one third of the surface of the rear stone in stage three of this arrangement is concealed because such a placement is essential for stability.

Fill the interstices with tightly packed earth, and plant azaleas, ferns, *Pieris japonica*, or *Enkianthus perulatus* in them. If the screen-style wall is to be used in water, however, fill with mortar in the submerged areas and with earth in all others.

Resembling the screen-style retaining wall, rows of stakes driven at the water's edge to prevent bank crumbling are especialy lovely combined with water iris and flags. Varying the heights and the number of rows of the stakes enlivens the arrangement (Fig. 240, bottom).

LEVEL MASONRY

Natural, flat-topped stones in gentle tiers of varied heights create a pleasing, stairstep retainer for slight inclines (Fig. 241). Section 2 of this figure shows the simplest three-stone version of this arrangement. These can be combined to form an interesting wall (3). Fig. 241-4 clearly reveals the stairstep nature of such settings, and though the bottom row of stones must be flat and have no dangerous projections, the upper rows can be of the so-called peeping form as long as they do not move when people walk on them. If the retaining effect is unimportant these stones can be used to create a harmonious and quiet ornamental group (Fig. 241-5). They must all have a certain variation in heights, but no drainage precautions are needed.

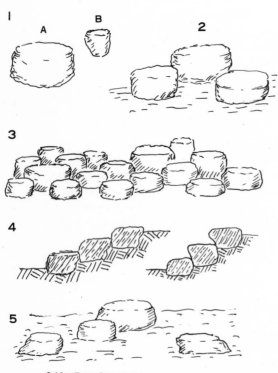

241. *Level masonry.*

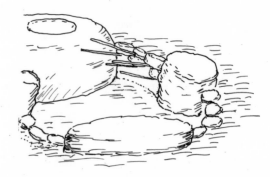

242. *Tortoise-shell-pattern work using small stones.*

D. Construction Order

First determine the topography of the garden, set the depth to which you will bury the roots of the stones, and then begin assembling the group. Stones requiring mechanical assistance must be set first and the smaller ones later. Waterfalls, rubble-work walls, tortoise-shell pattern walls, and other groups in which the construction order moves upward from the bottom become quickly soiled. After each days work, carefully clean them with a brush. To keep the outer surface or a rubble or tortoise-shell retaining wall straight and, if desired, to align the top stones, use cords tied to stakes set perfectly horizontal as guide lines. Selecting the stones for the top row is the most important point in carefully aligned walls. If they are not suitable, no matter how well placed all the others are, the wall will be a failure. Since it is essential to change the lower stones if the top ones are too high or too low, when you are about three rows from completion, begin to set the lower stones with a straight top in mind; this will lighten your later work. If the second row from the top is properly set the last one will be easy. With stones of roughly a foot in diameter, great care is not as important as with those as large as two or three feet in diameter.

Contrary to the preceding procedure, when arranging a small wall around the sea in front of a ritual water basin, begin with the top stones and work downward (Fig. 242). Hold the top stones in place with bamboo sticks or pieces of galvanized wire (one-quarter inch in diameter, one foot in length), and arrange stones below it. The bottom row may be buried in the ground if they are too large. Although this is more troublesome than setting from bottom to top, it makes perfect alignment of the top stones easier. Set the stones in place with mortar behind them—mixture of one part cement to three of sand—and leave openings at least one-half inch deep among the stones. Fill these cracks with moss before the mortar sets, and clean any mortar from the stone surfaces immediately.

E. Stone Steps

Most Western-style houses have no need of these, but I will include a few words on the topic for those who have incorporated deep Japanese eaves and verandas in their architectural plans.

In a sense something like a terrace, the stone step, or steps, modulates between the levels of the house and the garden and facilitates movement between the interior and the exterior.

In Japanese houses, the stone step should be about three inches narrower than the eave is deep to prevent it from being splashed with rainwater and about one-half as long as the room before which it is set. If longer, it establishes a bad proportional relationship. If the level of the veranda is only a foot or a foot and one-half higher than the ground, one stone will suffice. If it is more than two feet, however, two steps are needed. The veranda and the upper surface of the top stone step should be about ten inches apart; when other steps are used they should have a suitable rise. It is not necessary to set them all equal distances apart as long as they permit easy movement to and from the veranda level. The top stone, however, must be at least ten inches or one foot from the veranda to prevent troublesome spattering in rainy weather. When access is the only consideration, the stone step can be ten inches lower than the veranda, but if you intend to rest your feet on it as you sit on the veranda floor, as is the custom in Japan, increase the distance to about one foot. In Japanese-style houses, these stone should be set against the veranda supports.

The stone step for a *nijiriguchi* entrance to a teahouse should be from one foot to one foot three inches lower than the floor level and should be only about one foot four inches in diameter. In the section on the teahouse, I have already mentioned that this stone must be about five inches from the building. The stone step for the distinguished guests' entrance, though fundamentally identical with ordinary ones, should be less than three feet long.

F. Stepping Stones

The ideal average distance between stepping stones, based on a normal stride, is about four inches. This varies, of course, with the size of the stone: those with diameters of one foot are set about five inches apart, those of about ten inches are set seven inches apart. Stones of over one and one half feet in diameter are usually set to accommodate two steps (Fig. 243-G). Never place stones so that they require a stride of over one and one-half feet because of the resulting danger of slipping.

For back yards and areas where beauty is not paramount, stones may be set vertically, as in A of Fig. 243; but if aesthetic effect is important, the increased visual stability of the horizontal setting (B) is needed. Balance is lost if the axes of the stones all run diagonally in the same direction (C), but it is restored when one slants right while the next slants left (D). Of course, right-angle setting (B) presents no difficulties. When the stones are farther apart at one point than at others (E) no mutual relationship is established between them; however, they seem to be two halves of a single stone, when all opposing areas are roughly equidistant from each other. The setting in G uses large stones each of which requires two steps to cross.

In set distances—for instance from a teahouse to a gate or from the point of division in a path to a bridge—it is often necessary to decide whether to set one stone too many and crowd the arrangement or one stone too few and open it wide. Always choose the former method because, though less pleasing than a properly spaced plan, it is safer for walking.

By setting two stones vertically together and thus creating a certain variety, it is possible to accommodate an excess of stones without overcrowding (Fig. 244-A). Setting B illustrates the use of a large stone to indicate a division in a path. In all these diagrams, the lines indicate the movement of a person walking on the stones. The small stone to the right in B is supposed to provide a place for stepping aside when encountering another person on the same path; in fact, however, it is more often used to balance visually a setting when the spaces between stones are incorrect. Designed so that the pedestrian takes four steps then changes direction for three more, the setting in C must be made of moderately large stones because such a plan composed of stones of less than a foot in diameter gives an uneasy feeling similar to walking on a slender log. Unless small stones are in the staggered setting in Fig. 243-D, they are difficult to walk on.

Fig. 244-D, resembling a line of geese in flight, is the natural one for curved paths. The bottom three stones in the group should be reset as the dotted lines indicate to restore balance lost because all of the axes slant in the same direc-

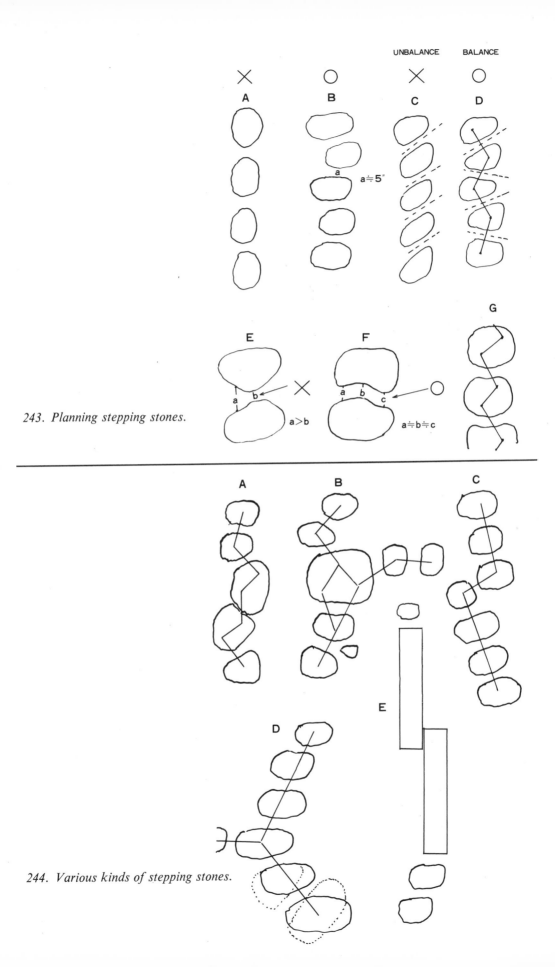

243. *Planning stepping stones.*

244. *Various kinds of stepping stones.*

tion. In this case also, unless the stones are one and one-half feet in diameter, the arrangement is uncomfortable for walking. Fig. 244-E illustrates a mixture of long rectangular and natural stones; I have already explained the overlap in rectangular stones.

Small stones generally provide the lightness of tone important to stepping-stone groups, but sometimes large (three or four feet in diameter) ones, set near the house, effectively balance a distant scene. Since the broad flat surface of the stones symbolize the spaciousness of the garden, as long as walking on them is comfortable they may be set as little as five inches or as much as one foot apart.

Generally, set stepping stones to project two or three inches above the surface of the ground. Although the higher setting is lovelier, the lower one is safer; allow the owner to decide which he prefers.

After making the necessary surface drainage arrangements and following your prepared plan, temporarily set the stepping stones in place. Level them by inserting pebbles or small bits of wood under the low parts. First walk over them to make sure they are comfortable; then move some distance away to examine them aesthetically. Make the necessary corrections, and lifting one at a time, dig out the amount of soil necessary to accommodate each stone. Do not raise them all from their temporary settings at one time and attempt to remember where and how they were placed; it is impossible. As you push soil under them with a small stick, keep a constant eye on their height from the ground, and make sure that their upper surfaces remain level. In the north, where freezing soil might wrench the stones out of place, dig the entire pathway to a depth of about four inches, spread it with gravel and then with sand, and finally, set the stepping stones on top of this drainage bed. It is also important to lay pipes in the gravel layer and to connect them with the general garden drainage system.

When the stones are in place, carefully clean them and the ground around them, but take pains not to disturb any interesting lichens or mosses growing on their surfaces.

G. Paving Stones

Though by no means an entirely Japanese garden feature, paving stones, as used in this country, have a few special characteristics that I should like to mention.

Fig. 245-A shows a formal Japanese paving arrangement of cut rectangular stones; this kind appears most often in front of ceremonious buildings in the *shoin* style. To produce the simple sophisticated beauty of this pavement it is important to use only T-shaped placements and to avoid X intersections, like those in E. Fig. 245-B effectively contrasts the soft textures of natural stones with the rigidity of rectangular ones and adds the charm of moss. Total harmony and balance unify the complexity of the all-natural-stone pavement in Fig. 245-C, where again, it is important to avoid X-shaped and radial intersections, like that in F, and to think of the T and the Y as basic patterns. The pavement in D, composed entirely of natural stones, goes one step farther toward informality by breaking up the carefully aligned edges of the preceding arrangement. Once again, avoid radial and X-shaped intersections, and do not set more than three—or in some rarer instances more than five—stones in a straight line. For example, the detached feeling of stones *a*, *b*, and *c* in Fig. 245-D disturbs the stability of

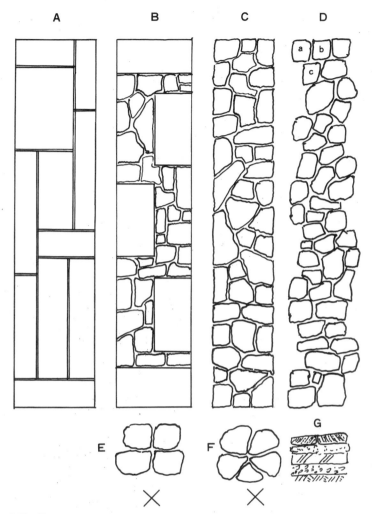

245. *Paving stones.*

the entire pavement. If I replaced these three stones with one large one, the problem would be solved.

The arrangement in C pleases because it combines irregular forms in a closely regulated pattern; that in D, however, charms by means of its unbounded freedom. It expresses most refined and subtle tastes. Always suit the kind of pavement to the mood of the garden.

Pavements B and C are most often made of thin stones. We use black cut stones for formal beauty or round rough textured stones when subtlety and wistful charm are intended.

When setting thin stones (cross section, Fig. 245-G), spread five inches of gravel first, pour three inches of concrete on top of that, and set the stones on the concrete with mortar. After putting them in place, fill in the cracks with cement mortar (1 : 2) to which has been added sufficent charcoal ash to create a color that harmonizes with the stones. The cracks should be at least one-half inch deeper than the surface of the stones in order to take advantage of the interesting shadows playing across them.

Stones of more than six inches in diameter and with considerable thickness will not move when walked on if they have a layer of sand and gravel under them. Stones of less than five inches in diameter may be set in place with mortar only.

Paved areas may be as wide as six feet in heavily traveled places—shrines, temples, public halls, hotels, restaurants, etc.—but one and one-half feet usually suffice for ordinary domestic gardens. Tea garden pavements are rarely more than two feet wide. Although the tops of the stones should be as high as those of stepping stones, with thin materials it is impossible to achieve a projection of more than one inch above the ground level because exposing the concrete under the stones destroys the effect of pavement.

Use cord lines to keep line pavements straight, and lay the stones with a watchful eye on uniform heights. For pavements like that in D, first draw the projected plan on the ground, and use a level to set the stones correctly. Try not to soil the tops of the stones with mortar, but should some get on them, brush it away before it hardens.

4. Constructing a Stream

For gardens blessed with abundant water, no special construction work is required, but unfortunately, such cases or so few that gardeners frequently must devise ways to introduce into their plans the refreshing sound of a flowing stream. In the series of scenes shown in Figs. 229 to 234 you see a stream overflowing with water and creating rivulets, eddys, still places, and finally a fall. This naturally blessed setting required no work to set the water in motion. It was, however, essential to raise the banks to a height of at least one foot to contain the water in its proper course.

Most often Japanese gardeners strive to do no more than create ripples on the surface of a stream—even a small one with low water level—because this gentle movement in a small garden produces the psychological effect of a rapidly flowing river. Merely spreading gravel (pieces of one inch in diameter) in the stream bed sets up rippling motion that symbolizes flowing waters. Generally, the slope of a garden stream should be a gentle 1/100, and it is most often S shaped; but it is always important to match the stream to the topography of the site.

To construct a garden stream, first plot the course by laying a rope along the ground. Examine it carefully and make needed corrections.

Next, drive stakes into the ground at each bend in the stream course, one stake on each side of each bend. Using a level, nail horizontal battens to these stakes so that they cross the stream and so that they are all at the same absolute height. Run a string from the middle of each batten to the middle of the next for the full length of the stream. If the bottom of the finished stream bed is two feet from the top of the batten at the source and if the distance from the source to the first bend is twenty feet on a 1/100 incline, the bottom of the completed bed at the first bend will be about two feet, two and one-half inches from the top of the batten at that point. As the section in Fig. 246 shows, the stream bed is composed of a total of nine and one-half inches of materials: four inches of concrete, four

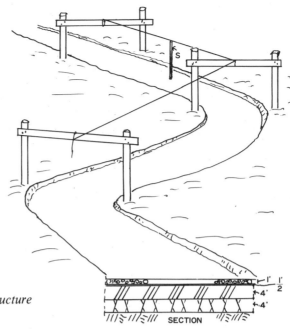

246. *Battens and temporary guide structure for stream construction.*

inches of rubble, one-half inch of mortar, and one inch of gravel; consequently the excavation depth at the source must be three feet from the top of the batten. Using this same system it is possible to calculate the excavation depth all along the course of the stream. To maintain a constant incline throughout the construction process, use a stick cut to the proper length, and measure with it all along the horizontal string. When the rubble has been spread, cut off four inches of the stick, and measure for the concrete. After the concrete has been poured, cut off four more inches of the stick, and measure for the following layer. Continue cutting the stick until all layers have been completed.

Begin digging the stream bed after the surrounding stone groups are complete. When you have spread the rubble on the bottom of the excavation and have packed it firmly, pour the concrete (a mixture of 1 : 3 : 6 or 1 : 2 : 4); follow this with a brushed-on layer of cement mortar (1 : 2) topped with a layer of uniform gravel. If the water flows along the top of the concrete, rushes will live. For this reason it is best to plant them before spreading the gravel.

Both because a constant incline of 1/100 is not always topographically feasible and because too much sameness is boring, vary the stream with falls, slow sections, rapids, of deep places where fish can be bred. In low-water streams, one inch of water above the gravel produces a satisfactory effect, but if the incline is too steep—1/20 or 1/30—the water will flow under the gravel and be invisible. In my comments on Figs. 96 and 97 I have already explained the advantage of filling the cracks among the pieces of gravel with mortar when the stream water is extremely scarce (see page 59).

If large stones on the bank concealing the gentle curves of the stream are part of your plan, use low ones (five inches) set to project into and recede from the water edge, and plant a half screen of rushes, or bamboo (*Sasa albo-marginata*). In such cases, set the stones when the concrete has been poured, and then add a mortar finish, because they could be forced out of place during the concrete pouring.

In deep areas, setting the stones after the concrete and the mortar have been applied provides increased protection from leakage. Make allowance for the roots of large stones by lowering the level of the concrete in the places where they are to stand.

5. Constructing a Pond

If natural water is near the surface and plentiful, estimate the average depth of the spring, determine the depth you need for the pond, lay out the outline of the pond with a rope, and construct a set of battens (see section on the stream, page 142) that help you dig to the proper depths. As a construction convenience, dig one area of the pond deeper than the rest, and use a pump to force the natural waters into it so that work on the other sections will not slow down because of inundation. If one area of the garden is naturally lower than the pond, at the beginning, lay drainage pipes to carry the water away until the pond is complete. Should the pond be too large for drainage pipes alone a pump will be essential.

Drive concrete pilings where stones are to be set, spread rubble on top of them, and pour four inches (from six to seven inches if the pond is large or if heavy stones are to used) of concrete on top of these. Wait until the concrete has thoroughly hardened before beginning the stone group. Although reinforced concrete is extremely safe in most cases, unless the pond is at least one-thirtieth of an acre, it is unnecessary. Furthermore, if the ground base sinks, even reinforced concrete cannot prevent cracking. Should the danger of sinkage exist, the concrete pilings must be driven deep enough to reach the hard lower strata of the ground base. A pleasing and safe pond can also be made without stone edges or pilings by cutting the banks to a gentle thirty-degree incline and planting Dutch rushes or reeds at the borders.

Even when ground water is too deep to be conveniently used, if a nearby constant supply of water is available, following the procedure outlined above, first set the stones, and then either pour concrete on the pond bottom or back it and the cracks among the stones with mortar or clay.

The ponds I have just described are sufficient for gardens with abundant supplies of natural water, but if you must rely on city water, completely leak-proof construction is necessary. Once again, first lay out the shape of the pond on the ground with a rope, construct horizontal battens, establish the proper depths for the pond, lay drainage pipes, and dig so that the bottom of the pond slopes toward the drainage outlet (incline of about 1/200). Next spread and pack firmly a layer of rubble on the pond bottom, and then add a layer of finer gravel. Spread the border areas—the parts of the bottom that will eventually be under the pond walls,—with a layer of crushed concrete about one foot and four inches in depth. Erect the framework for the concrete walls on top of this layer: the upper surface must be horizontal, and the walls are usually about four inches thick. The concrete mixture should be 1 : 3 : 6.

After about two days, when the concrete has set sufficiently, remove the formwork, and pour a layer of concrete, mixed to the same proportions, on the pond bottom. This should be about four inches thick if the pond is less than one-sixtieth of an acre in area and from six to seven inches if the pond is larger.

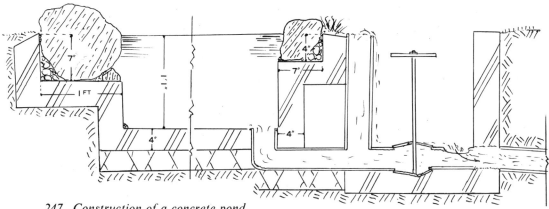

247. *Construction of a concrete pond.*

Allow a day to pass; then paint a one-half-inch layer of cement mortar on both the sides and the bottom. If the sand used in this mortar is sifted and fine, it may be unnecessary, but a good waterproofing material increases the safety of the pond. Cover the concrete with plastic or a tarpaulin to protect it from the direct sun as it dries.

The pond in Fig. 247—less than one-sixtieth of an acre in area—is deep enough (about one foot) to raise carp or goldfish, and the deeper area of about three feet square protects the fish from freezing in severe cold or from suffering in great heat.

Inclining the pond walls slightly to the outside allows ice on the surface to slip upward and thus helps prevent cracks in the concrete. In the pond in the illustration, however, the shelf-like areas for small ornamental stones serve a similar function and permit the use of perfectly perpendicular pond walls. As the chart shows, the depths of the shelves must vary to accommodate the stones to be set on them; very large stones may be set directly on the pond bottom.

Mortar applied between the stone's bottom and the concrete of the pond prevents slippage, even in earthquakes, and small rocks or pieces of concrete inserted between the stone and the wall of the pond and then coated with mortar prevent earth from slipping behind the stone and forcing it out of place.

Since pond water is usually dirtier at the bottom, instead of constructing overflows that drain away the clean upper levels, construct a siphon arrangement (Fig. 247), which drains off the unclean bottom water and thereby creates a more healthful environment for the fish. For times when excess rainfall or heavy intakes of water make it essential, a top overflow, about one-half inch higher than the average level of the water is useful. The bottom drainage opening should be at about the level shown in Fig. 247.

Never set the stones at the edge or in the middle of the pond until the concrete has been poured, the mortar applied, and the entire arrangement dried, because setting them prematurely will cause trouble should leakage ever require repair.

It might happen, however, that a large stone already in the area would improve the pond if left as it is. In such cases, brush the stone surface thoroughly, and before pouring the concrete paint a mixture of cement and water over the areas that will come in contact with the concrete. This will force the air from the minute cavities in the stone surface and promote a waterproof adhesion between

249. *Border of grasses.*

stone and concrete. Unfortunately, putting the stones in place after the concrete is set makes final finishing extremely difficult, but it is better than running the risk of serious leakage once the pond is complete. Finally, since you will have to use tripods with chain blocks to set the stones, tie the legs of the tripod firmly in place to prevent their slipping and damaging the concrete.

Insert small stones behind the large ones, once the setting is correct, and brush on the mortar when the stone group is finished. Round pebbles spread on the bottom of the finished pond are lovely, but since they require a certain amount of care, omit them if you wish. The concrete of the pond bottom will assume the color of natural rock in one or two years.

Ponds without stone or pile edgings are lovely trimmed with rushes, set in the small shelf that must be prepared during the laying of the pond walls (Fig. 248). A finished example of such a pond with a grassy knoll at its edge is shown in Fig. 249.

6. Setting Stone Lanterns and Towers

Since the basic function of a stone lantern is to light, its lamp compartment must be directed toward the space it is intended to illuminate. This does not

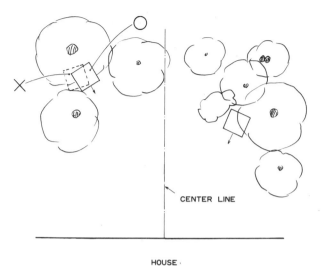

250. *Sellecting the proper direction for a stone lantern.*

DIREC-TION	E UN	W KIRIKU	S TARAKU	N AK
KONGO-KAI	𑀊	𑀊	𑀊	𑀊
	A	AN	Ā	AK
TAIZO-KAI	𑀊	𑀊	𑀊	𑀊
		AMIDDHA BUDDHA		
		畢 昴 胃		

251. *Figure of Buddha and letters engraved on a stone tower and directions in which the tower must face.*

mean, however, that it must squarely face the room onto which the garden opens. In fact, such a placement suggests a photograph of a married couple who, though close together, seem widely separated because they face each other directly. Instead, set a stone lantern in the right side of the garden so that its lamp compartment faces slightly left and one on the left so that the compartment is turned slightly to the right (Fig. 250). In the setting indicated by the dotted square on the left, the foliage of the trees in front obscures the lantern.

The lantern in Fig. 31 is intended to light a spacious lawn and to suggest fishermen's lures in the shadowy area leading to the sea. Those in Figs. 38 and 106 illuminate ritual water basins, whereas those in Figs. 42, 52, 107, and 130 reflect in the waters of ponds. The lantern in Fig. 47 sheds light on a footpath, and the one in Fig. 149 brightens an entranceway.

Towers, too, should be set with their fronts directed as are the lamp compartments of lanterns, but when they bear Buddhist figures or Sanscrit inscriptions, there are certain fixed method for setting them. Although some people say that the same is true of lanterns ornamented with carved openings representing stars or moons, this is not always pertinent; and the best plan is to suit the lantern setting to the needs of the garden.

Buddhas are believed to reside in individual points of the compass; consequently, sides of stone towers, or pagodas—originally Buddhist reliquary towers—bearing carved figures or Sanscrit letters pertinent to a certain Buddha must be set to face the direction associated with that Buddha. Inscriptions associated with two realms—wisdom and virtue (*Kongokai*) and reason (*Taizokai*)—are set to face as shown in Fig. 251. Although towers of the Kongokai type are more common, I include settings for both kinds because of the similarlity in the inscriptions for AK (north) of *Kongokai* and A (east) of *Taizokai*. The figure of Buddha represented seated with his hands in his lap is usually Amiddha Nyorai; it is safe to set this figure facing west, the region in which Amiddha is believed to dwell. Set these Chinese characters 畢 昴 胃 facing west when the pagoda bears representations of the twelve Oriental zodiacal signs.

In recent years, certain pagodas with figures of the same Buddha on all four sides have appeared on the commercial market. Set them so that they look good; nothing else matters in these cases.

The process of setting both stone lanterns and ornamental pagodas is much the same. First dig a depression, then put a layer of rubble in the bottom of it, pack firmly, add a layer of gravel, and pack firmly again. The hole should be deep enough that when the rubble and gravel are in place and the bottom section of the lantern or tower set, its lowest part will be concealed. Although it depends to some extent on the type of base the lantern or tower has, in most cases a hole four inches deep suffices.

Stone lanterns are composed of all or some of the following six parts: jewel, roof, lamp compartment, central base, trunk, and base; stone pagodas of the following: the *kūrin*, or air circle, and several series of roofs and lamp compartments, and finally a base. They may have as many as thirteen and as few as three sets of roofs and lamp compartments. When they are more numerous, there is ususally a trunk section and some intermediary stones between them and the base. The five basic divisions of these towers are a clear representation of the five Oriental elements: air wind, fire, water, and earth. Two special types of tower the *Tahoto* and the *Hokyointo*, are similar in nature and set in the same way.

In erecting comparatively light towers or lanterns of less than six feet in height, after preparing the foundation described above, set the base (the earth ring) and the next section (the water ring), and check for level. If they are untrue, raise them with a lever and insert gravel where needed.

For lamps, next add the trunk section and, using a bob, check for vertical plumb. Use gravel again for necessary corrections. Although it is possible to use bits of lead or iron instead, gravel is preferable because moss can be used to conceal it later. Next add the intermediary base, and once again check for level and plumb; and make sure that this section projects evenly from all the others. Finally, put the lamp compartment, roof, and jewel on top. Use a platform, if the lantern is too tall for the person working to reach the top, or if the lamp compartment is light, first set the roof on the intermediary base, then have an assistant put the lamp compartment in place as you hold the roof up for him.

The winch, block, and chain, or the wrecker crane must serve for stone ornaments of more than eight feet in height. Care must be taken in tying lines to them, however, to insure that the edges and surfaces are not damaged. For instance, a smooth lantern trunk must be tied separately front and back (Fig. 252-A), or the rope will slip upward. The rough trunk in B, on the other hand, need be tied as in A only on one side and the rope brought around to the other side and passed through the other end. Although some few careless gardeners put sticks or ropes through the lamp compartments of lanterns to raise them, this should never be done because the danger of damage to the stone is great. Nevertheless, because the rope will get caught on the intermediary base if it is brought up from below, when using a wrecker or a chain and block to raise the stone in a position similor to its final setting, tie as shown in Fig. 252-A. Leave an opening only as large

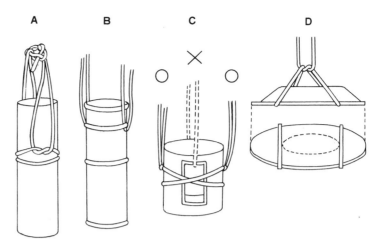

A　　　　　B　　　　　C　　　　　D

252. Using heavy rope to assemble a stone lantern.

as the diameter of the lamp compartment, and tie as in the chart showing the back of the roof (D). Protect the surface of the stone from the cables and chains with burlap.

A properly packed lantern or tower will bear small markings on the back showing how they should be combined.

When the lantern is in place, set a flat stone, from four to eight inches in diameter, slightly to the outside and from one to two feet in front of it. The size and height of the tower or lantern governs the size of the front stone, but there is no need to go to the extent of using a stone three feet high in front of a very tall lantern. In all cases, one foot of height is sufficient for the front stone; if the lantern is huge, use a stone with a large diameter.

Although stone towers gain dignity with added height, stone lanterns are designed to give the impression that their lamp compartments are on eye level. Too much height not only spoils the mood of even a wonderful lantern, it clearly shows that the person who set it did not understand the stone cutter's art.

After completing the setting, brush away all dust and dirt, and sprinkle it with water. To intensify the rich beauty of natural stones materials in these ornaments, it is essential to water them daily.

LANTERN TYPES

The hundreds of kinds of lanterns widely used in Japanese gardens cannot be listed here, but I have selected a few that are based on masterpieces of the lamp-cutter's art and experience (Fig. 253). The photograph is of a collection of lanterns in the lot of a dealer in garden materials.

A. Kasuga style, B. Sangatsudo style, C. Hannyaji style, D. Uzumasa style, E. Rengeji style, F. Nishinoya style, and G. Byodoin style, frequently used, are suitable for setting among a stand of trees where the branches partly conceal them. The chart indicates the names of each part of the lantern. Notice that the Byodoin style has a distinctive lamp compartment made of two standing stone panels. H. Yukimi style, I. Tamate style, J. Kotoji style, and K. Mino style (also called Korakuen style) are for use at the water's edge. Since these are intended to shed light on water they need not be partly concealed by branches and leaves. The Tamate style is set on stones. All of these can also be used to light foot paths. L. Chosen style, M. Oribe style, N. Mizubotaru style, O.

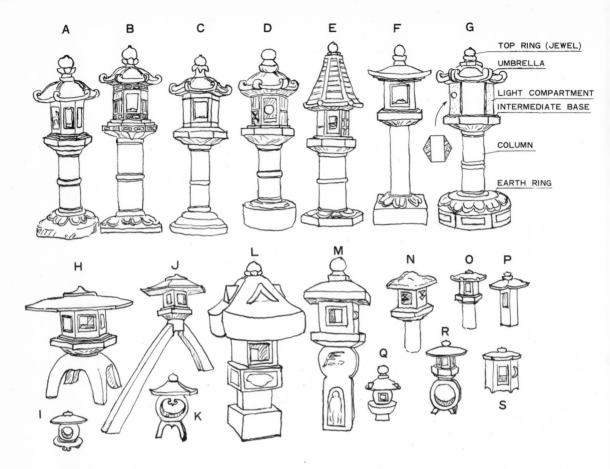

TOP RING (JEWEL)
UMBRELLA
LIGHT COMPARTMENT
INTERMEDIATE BASE
COLUMN
EARTH RING

253, 253-a. Primary types of stone lanterns.

Soeki style (also called the Roji style), and P. Koetsu style are for use at the ritual water basin. In keeping with the required refined mood these lanterns are best semi-conceaed with foliage. The Mizubotaru style is often used at the edges of ponds.

Q. Rakugan style, and R. Omokage style are for use on ornamental beaches. The Rakugan lantern, since it symbolizes a flight of geese alight, should be set on a flat beach.

Small lanterns of this kind are set at the side of the entrance or stepping stones of a teahouse or on a platform stone.

TOWER TYPES (Fig. 254)

Gojunoto—available in five- and three-story types, this pagoda sometimes rests on a base stone instead of legs.

Juichisoto—This eleven-storied pagoda, or its related three-, seven-, nine-, and thirteen-storied versions, often bears either carvings of a Buddha or of Sanscrit inscriptions on all four sides of the trunk section.

Tahoto—The charactistic of a Tahoto is a massive trunk section. These sometimes have higher bases than the one in the photograph.

Hokyointo—Possibly because it resembles a Buddhist grave marker, this tower is less often used in gardens than the other kinds. The base is frequently high, making the resemblance to a grave stone more striking. The roof shape and ornament distinguish it sharply from other towers.

254. Primary types of stone towers.

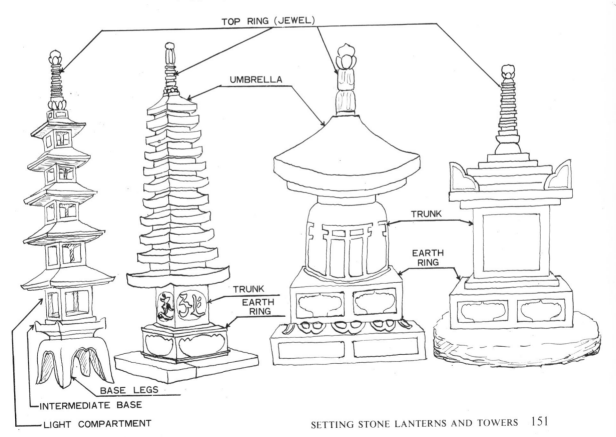

7. Setting the Ritual Water Basin

Ocurring in two main types, ritual water basins are usually set in one of two traditional placements. The *shoin*-style basin, named for the famous Japanese architectural style often used in formal rooms in residences, is generally a tall, urn-shaped basin and is set much like the wash basins outside of toilets. The low *tsukubai* ritual water basin, designed primarily for the tea garden, derives its name from the Japanese verb *tsukubau* (to crouch) because it is impossible to use these basins unless one assumes that position. Figs. 13, 37, 106, and 256-A show examples.

The settings for them are with an open depression of level area (called the sea) in front of the basin or with an equal amount of flat area all around the basin: the former is called the distant setting and the latter (Fig. 256-B) the middle setting.

Basins carved in regular shapes by artificial means—with the exception of the Hashigui style—usually employ middle setting because they are designed so that their lower sections must be buried in the ground. Since it seemed a pity to bury the basin in Fig. 256, however, I set it on a base stone. The Hashigui style (Fig. 259-I) is another example of a basin that may be advantageously set on a base stone.

Begin a middle setting by digging a hole so deep that when the basin is in place its top will be approximately twelve inches above the level of the surrounding ground. Place any necessary base stones in the bottom of the hole, add the basin, and using a level, check the horizontality of the entire arrangement.

After having filled the basin eight-tenths full of water, using the bottom of a laddle, press the water surface to cause an overflow (Fig. 255). Basins with carefully cut, perfectly level rims should overflow evenly in all directions. Those with rough rims or with cut depressions in the top must be set to overflow in the front only. Correct unequal or faulty overflow by inserting stones under the basin where needed.

The stone in front of the basin should be about two inches higher than the stepping stones leading to it and, therefore, about ten inches lower than the rim of the basin. A distance of about two feet should separate its leading edge from the forward edge of the water (Fig. 256). A stone for a candle should be on the left of the front stone far enough away that a person crouching on the front stone can easily reach it. On the right, at a similar distance, should be another stone, this one intended to hold a bucket of hot water placed there for use in winter (Fig. 256-B). Their heights should be as indicated in the chart. For the

255. *Establishing the level for a ritual water basin.*

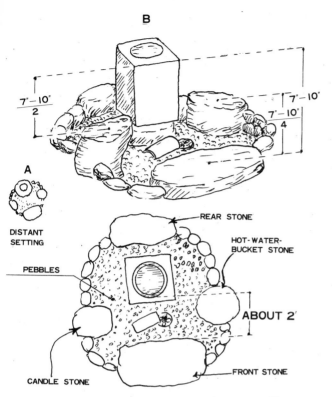

B

7"-10"/2

7"-10"/4

7"-10"

A

DISTANT
SETTING

PEBBLES

REAR STONE

HOT-WATER-
BUCKET STONE

ABOUT 2'

CANDLE STONE

FRONT STONE

256. Arranging the front of a centrally
placed basin.

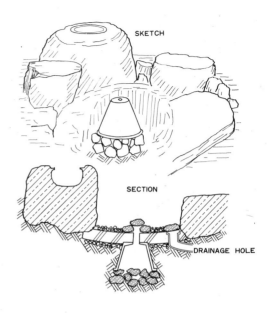

SKETCH

SECTION

DRAINAGE HOLE

257. Drainage pit in front of a ritual water
basin.

sake of visual balance, a middle setting often requires a back stone, although, if the available space is cramped, it may be omitted (Fig. 256).

When these primary stones are in place, fill in the spaces among them with a retaining wall of smaller stones (from four to ten inches in diameter). With formal carved basins use the tortoise-shell masonry pattern and the natural rubble work design with natural stone ones.

Following the directions in Fig. 257, dig the sea to a depth of about one foot. Spread gravel on the bottom, invert a large flower pot on top of the gravel, and fill the depression in again. Insert a stick in the hole of the flower pot to prevent its being blocked, and pour concrete in the bottom of the sea. When the concrete has partly hardened, turn the stick around a few times so that it will not adhere to the pot and will be easily removable later. Spread gravel of a uniform one- or two-inch grain on the hardened concrete after you have thoroughly cleaned the sea area, and conceal the opening to the drainage pit with a few slightly larger stones. If the sea of the basin flows off into a small stream or if you have built another drainage pipe, the flower-pot drain is unnecessary. The diameter of the hole at the top of the drainage pit should be smaller than that of the pit because cylindrical or semi-circular openings produce the effect of deep water and a resulting gloom.

Fig. 258 shows an *oritsukubai* sunken in a deeper area and approached by a short flight of stone steps. In these arrangements (discussed in the section on the

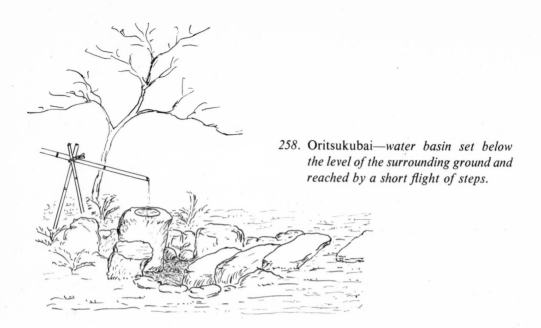

258. Oritsukubai—*water basin set below the level of the surrounding ground and reached by a short flight of steps.*

tea garden) it is usual to employ tall basins and flumes that suggest piping in fresh water from distant mountains. The bottom step should be wide so that a person crouching on it does not bump his hips into the step above.

STYLES OF RITUAL WATER BASINS

Fig. 259 shows a few of the many different styles of ritual water basins. A and B are both natural stone shapes with holes cut in the top for water; the former is tall enough for use as a *shoin*-type basin, the later is suited to a *tsukubai* basin. In setting both, the bottoms must be buried slightly in the ground. A section of an old pagoda with a hole cut in the top for water, the basin in C has carvings of Buddhas on all four sides. Six-sided versions are available. Although the ones made from old stone pagodas are often very expensive, less costly reproductions are on the market. Because the Fusen basin (D) is thin, it should be set on a thick base stone to stand about six or seven inches higher than the front stone. The sea in front of it should be deeper than usual. If drainage requirements make a shallow sea desirable, set the basin directly on the gravel without a base stone.

Somewhat similar in shape, the basin in J is a reproduction of one in the front garden of the famous temple Ryoan-ji, in Kyoto. The inscription "*Ware tada tariru o shiru*" admonishes Man to refrain from attempts to fulfill many hopes and to be satisfied with poverty; this kind of basin is widely used.

The simple Natsume urn in E is generally used as a *shoin* basin as is that in F, a copy of the so-called Ginkaku-ji basin in the gardens of the renowned Temple of the Silver Pavilion, also in Kyoto. Another *shoin*-style basin the *shiogama* urn (G) is a replica of pots used long ago to bake salt. Called a Yugyoku basin when in the proportions shown in H, the same shape, when slightly taller and known as a Teppatsu is an adapted section of the trunk of a stone pagoda. All of these basins use base stones.

The Hashigui (bridge piling) basin shown in I is most often used in small gardens. The natural boulder in K contains the water in a naturally formed depression.

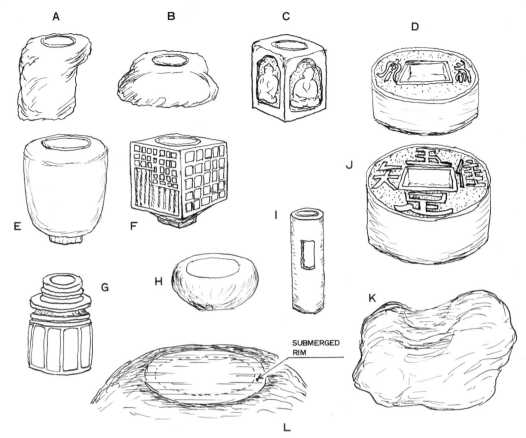

259. *Primary types of ritual water basin.*

Fig. 259-L illustrates the shelf-like ridge, just inside the outer rim of the water hole, that, submerged to a depth of one-fourth to one-eighth of an inch, creates the impression of overflowing water.

FLUMES AND *SOZU*

Used to lead water from a vertical pipe into the water basin, the Koma flume (Fig. 260-A) consists of a bamboo casing around the water pipe, a small box (*koma*) at the top of the bamboo casing, and a section of rubber hose leading from the end of the pipe into a length of bamboo, which has some thin dividing sections left partly intact to cause the water to dance into the basin about seven or eight inches below. The hose connection (see section in Fig. 260-A) is needed only if the box itself in not completely waterproof.

Designed to carry water from distance places, the *nagatoi* flume in B suggests distant mountains and rural retreats; the *bokutoi* in C replaces the bamboo pipes with a section of partly rotted log.

The *sozu* is a device invented many ages ago by farmers to frighten deer and birds that damaged crops. Water flowing from the source along a pipe falls into a short section of bamboo pipe, suspended on a pin and closed at the bottom end with the natural bamboo membrane. When the short section becomes full, the weight of the water tips the open end down, thus emptying the water. The closed end then swings quickly down and strikes a log or stone set to catch

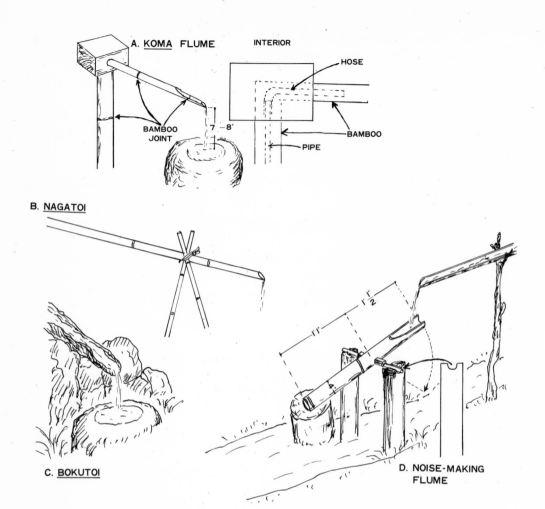

A. KOMA FLUME

INTERIOR

HOSE

BAMBOO
JOINT

7 — 8'

BAMBOO

PIPE

B. NAGATOI

C. BOKUTOI

D. NOISE-MAKING
FLUME

260. Kakehi *flume and* sozu *(noise-making) flume.*

it. The resulting sharp clack is supposed to alarm the marauding animals and put them to flight. In tea gardens, the *tsukubai* ritual basin is placed to catch the water spilled from the tipping bamboo pipe.

8. Garden Paths and Staircases

Certainly, when economy of motion is paramount, a straight line from one point to another is most desirable, but for purposes of relaxation, a curving garden path requiring one hundred steps to cover the distance easily transversed in thirty, calms the stroller and leads him, without his conscious volition, along a pleasing path. For this reason most of the garden examples in this book use straight, efficient paths near houses and rambling ones in the more spacious garden areas.

Gravel spread on walkways is beautiful, but it can work its way into neighboring areas of lawn and cause serious maintenance problems.

In addition to providing dry passage over wet grass and protecting lawn and mosses from being walked on, paths must also serve the psychological function of inviting the stroller to enjoy his walk. Although hotels and public parks sometimes employ paths as wide a six feet, in most Japanese gardens the mountain footpath style of one and one-half to three feet is preferred.

One of the best path compositions is a layer of rough gravel with an under layer of coarser (one-quarter of an inch) gravel topped with well rolled fine sand, but other interesting arrangements include bricks or paving stones set far enough apart to allow the planting of grass in the cracks among them.

Staircases may be made of large stones or of logs held in place with small stakes, or they may be an interesting application of the large roots of trees growing beside the path.

In general, paths and staircases are constructed alike in both Japan and the West.

9. Bridges

The following illustrations show a few of the many bridges popularly used in Japanese gardens.

The bridge with handrail (Fig. 261) is probably best represented by the famous Gojo Bridge in Kyoto and the Shin-kyo at Nikko. People intending to use this bridge would do well to order the ornamental bronze fittings from Japan.

The combination wisteria trellis and bridge in Fig. 262 creates a refreshing cool relaxation spot beside a pond.

Carefully selected natural stones with a proper bow can be chipped and cut

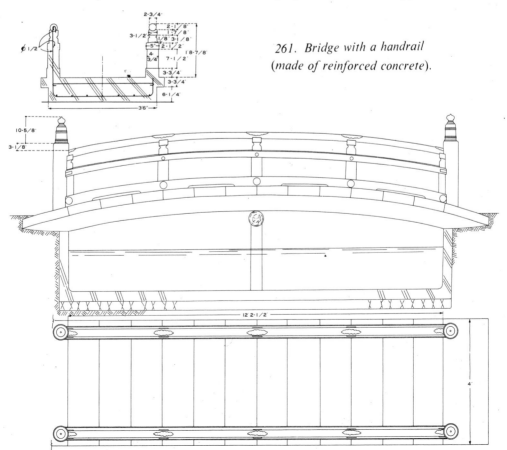

*261. Bridge with a handrail
(made of reinforced concrete).*

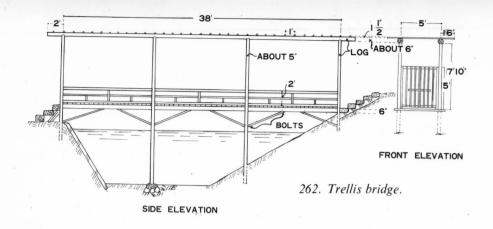

262. *Trellis bridge.*

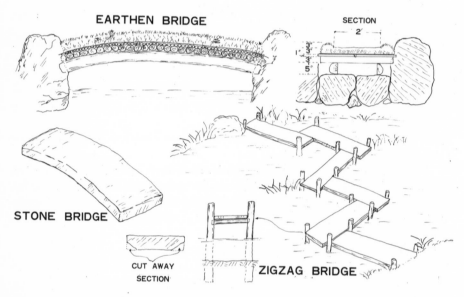

263. *Stone bridge, earthen bridge, zigzag bridge.*

to form stone bridges of great beauty. Trimming the ends of the stones as shown in the section in Fig. 263 improves the stability of the setting.

Although the Yatsubashi (a zigzag bridge) in Fig. 263, derives its name from its original eight sections, any number of large flat stones can be set on frames consisting of pilings with cross pieces to form this pleasing and relaxing bridge (Fig. 103).

Earthen bridges require a single log, with a proper bow, cut into two pieces lengthwise and set to form the main supports. On top of these are placed cut logs, and on top of them cut pieces of bamboo, trimmed so that the joints are invisible. To prevent the earth from leaking through, spread a galvanized lead or plastic sheet on top of the bamboo, and then add the proper thickness of earth. The edges of the path thus formed should be higher than its center and should bear ornamental planting of something like *Arenaria* sandwort.

10. Patterns in Raked Gravel

Although the greenery of a garden is soothing to the nerves and easy on the eyes, sometimes highlighting rocks and other garden elements with white, black, brown, or blue gravel raked into patterns adds important contrast.

Dig to a depth of about eight inches, spread a layer of rubble about three and one-half inches thick, add another layer of finer gravel (about one to one-half inches in diameter) followed by a thin layer of river sand (less than one-half inch in diameter). On top of this spread the ornamental gravel for raking (grain of about one-quarter of one inch). For a still safer base that will keep out grasses·and weeds, top a two-inch layer of gravel with three inches of concrete.

The grain of the gravel for the patterns is largely a matter of taste, but it should be coarse enough to resist the wind. In Japan from one-third to one-quarter of an inch is usual. Weathered granite gravel, like that available in the Yosemite National Park in the United States, is almost identical with the Shirakawa gravel used in the famous Kyoto gardens. I feel sure that similar gravels are available in most other countries.

The layer of gravel for raking should be about three inches thick, and the color depends on the surroundings: in bright sunny areas blue and brown reduce the glare, whereas white gravel brightens shady places.

Simply spread smooth on the ground, gravel emphasizes the good points of buildings and plants around it, but raked into simple patterns it seems to come alive itself. Although an ordinary rake will serve, we make a special tool by cutting jagged protrusions in a board seven inches wide, one-half inch thick, and about one and one-half feet long and attaching a five-foot handle to it.

The simplest pattern is a single rake's width of lines surrounding and running parallel with buildings and other large garden elements, but there are a number of other more complicated patterns including the fish-scale, the blue waves, and the whirlpool. Raked gravel should produce a mood of freshness and simplicity; therefore, the patterns should never be fussy or excessively ornamental.

Large gravel (diameters of three or four inches) can be arranged in impressive patterns for small courtyard gardens, but cleaning leaves and trash from among the stones is more difficult than the simple raking that suffices to keep a garden of smaller-grain gravel in good condition.

11. Fences and Gates

Generally speaking, fences fall into three types: the main outer fence dividing the private world of the house and garden from the outside, the inner fences that separate the functionally different sections of the garden, and small projecting partitions jutting out from the corners of buildings (*sode-gaki*). I will dismiss the outer fence here; it is largely a matter of protection and is little . used in the United States, but I will offer a few examples of inner fences for the information of those who would like to add one to their gardens simply for the mood.

I have avoided fences requiring the use of the special ropes, common in Japan, but only available abroad upon special importation.

Fences

BAMBOO TILE FENCE
Erect a framework by burying fence posts two feet in the ground and running

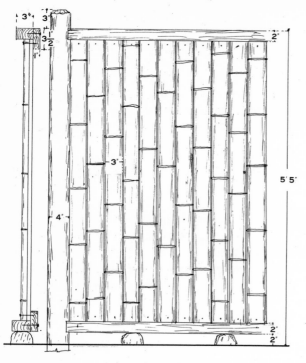

264. *Bamboo tile fence.*

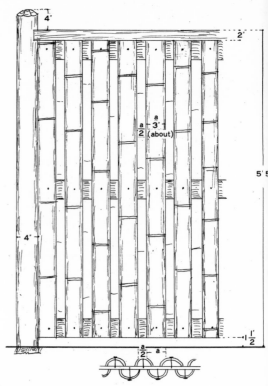

265. *Bamboo with wide braces.*

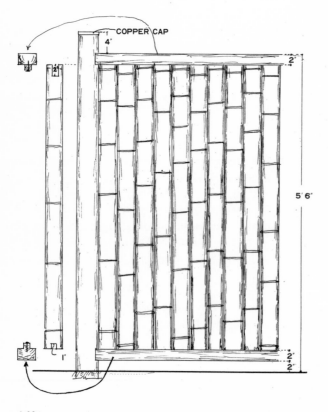

266. *Fence of unsplit bamboo.*

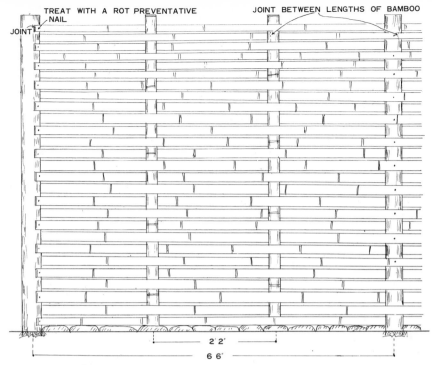

2' 2"

6' 6'

267. *Weir fence.*

horizontal members, one at the top and one about two inches from the ground. To both of these are added other horizontals to form an L-shaped section. After splitting large pieces of bamboo in half and removing the dividing membranes, nail them to the vertical projections of the horizontal timbers so that they overlap like mission tiles (see Fig. 264). Notice that one piece is placed, top end (narrow) up and its neighbor top side down.

The joints of the individual pieces should be staggered.

BAMBOO WITH WIDE BRACES

After erecting a framework consisting of posts buried two feet and wide top, middle, and bottom braces with an extra horizontal piece on the inner side of the top brace, nail the pieces of bamboo first to the front and then to the back of the braces to create a continuous line of convex and concave surfaces (see Fig. 265). Though this requires a little more bamboo than the following fence, it completely shuts out views from the opposite side while nonetheless allowing the passage of a certain amount of air.

FENCE OF UNSPLIT BAMBOO

Bury the fence posts, and attach the small wooden strips to the top and bottom horizontal members (see Fig. 266). Cut notches in large pieces of unsplit bamboo. Attach the lower horizontal; then insert the bamboo with lower notch downward. Finally, add the upper horizontal which fixes the bamboo in place. All of the pieces should be upside down, that is the reverse of their natural growing position. This means that though the top of the fence is tightly closed, there are slight gaps between the palings at the bottom. An interesting open fence results from leaving one paling width open between pieces of bamboo.

WEIR FENCE

Erect main support posts at distances of six feet and six inches, and add minor bamboo support posts at distances of two feet and two inches. Using either split bamboo or unsplit one-inch bamboo, weave the pieces among the supports as shown in Fig. 267. Fences of this kind, originally used as earth retainers, are rustic and lovely made with small branches instead of bamboo.

KOREAN PALISADE
Three wide braces are woven alternately over and under six or seven one-inch strips of split bamboo. For fences designed to be seen from one side only, turn all the bamboo strips bark outward, but for those that are viewed from both sides, create a color contrast by turning one set of six or seven strips bark inward and its neighboring set bark outward. Since bamboo splits easily, make holes in it with a gimlet before nailing it to the upper and lower horizontal braces.

OPEN PALISADE
Although also employing three wide braces, the fence in Fig. 269 is light and witty because of the greatly reduced number of vertical bamboo strips. The amount of projection of the vertical above the horizontal is determined by means of the simple expedient of multiplying the diameter of the support post by one-half, one, one and one-half, or two.

TWO-BRACE OPEN FENCE
The two braces in the fence in Fig. 270, pass through slits cut in the intermediate support posts. The unsplit bamboo nailed alternately to the inside and outside of the braces at distances of about five or six inches does not rot as fast as in some other fences because it does not directly contact the earth. A favorite variation of this fence, generally used as a partition between garden areas, replaces the bamboo verticals with living *Dendropanax trifidus* or *Nandina domestica* tied to the braces.

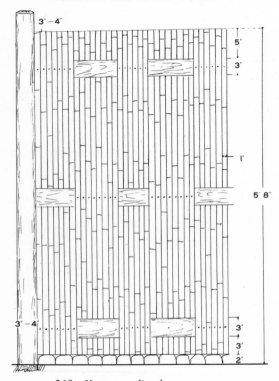

268. *Korean palisade.*

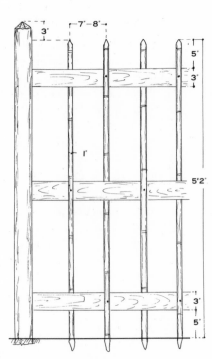

269. *Open palisade.*

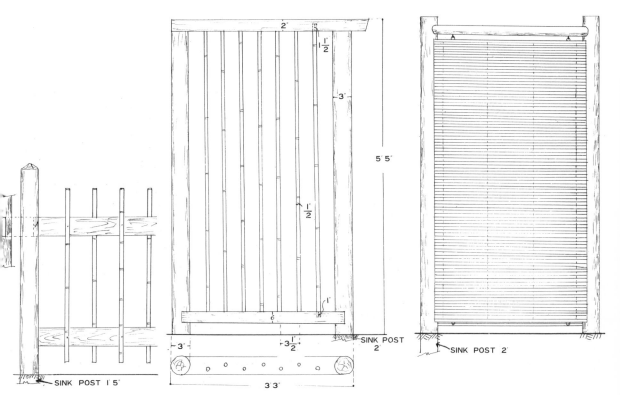

270. Two-brace open fence.　　　*271. Bamboo lattice fence.*　　　*272. Bamboo-blind fence.*

Partitioning Fence Sections "Sodegaki"

The next few fences belong to a category used in Japan at the corners of buildings to block views and to partition partially. Although generally attached to the shutter boxes common in all Japanese homes, but unknown in the West, they can serve Occidental gardens by creating a wind screen, concealing something unsightly, or simply adding a touch of Japanese flavor to the setting. Their standard measurements are five feet five inches in height and three feet in width.

BAMBOO LATTICE FENCE

Though useless as a concealing partition, this fence adds considerable elegance to its surroundings. It is made by sinking two wooden posts in the ground for support and running horizontal upper and lower braces as shown in Fig. 271. The palings are unsplit bamboo about one inch in diameter. Holes must be cut in the upper and lower horizontal members to hold the bamboo in place: because the hole in the upper is deeper than that in the lower each paling can be set by inserting the top end first, to the extent of the depth of the hole, and then lowering it in to place in the proper hole in the lower horizontal.

BAMBOO-BLIND FENCE

Placed between garden sections this simple bamboo blind hung by hooks from a horizontal can be raised or lowered as the occasion demands. Additional hooks at the bottom hold the blind in place.

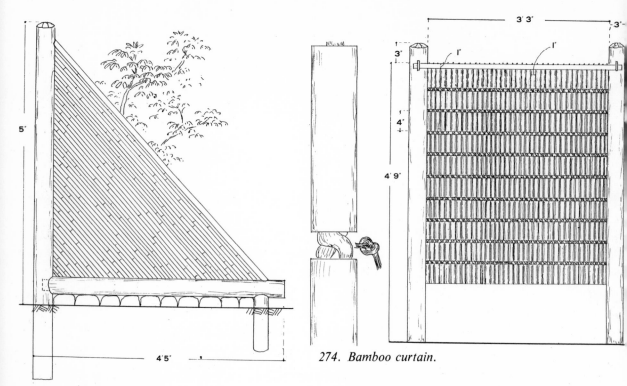

273.. Harp fence.

274. Bamboo curtain.

HARP FENCE
Tightly closed at the bottom but open at the top where camellias or winter camellias show to good effect, this simple fence requires one vertical log support, and one horizontal log base either nailed to or trimmed and inserted into the vertical. The outer end of the log base rests on a piling sunk in the ground. Set the bamboo diagonals by either cutting a groove in the vertical and horizontal to carry them or by nailing them in place. A fence of this kind is too bright and showy for a tea garden.

BAMBOO CURTAIN
Similar to the beaded curtains of the Mediterranean, but more subtle in coloring, this bamboo curtain (Fig. 274) both partitions and serves as a doorway. It is made by cutting many four- or five-inch lengths of bamboo so that the joints do not show and running a rope through them. Tie each section off as the chart indicates, and hang the finished bead-like chains close together from the top horizontal of the framework. The curtain should stop about one foot from the ground. Make the framework high enough to walk under.

BROKEN WORK FENCES
Since all of these fences structurally require tying with a special black rope—available through import only—I show the proper way to make the four-pronged knot traditional to such fences in Fig. 275. A′ in step 1 becomes A″, A‴, and A⁗ in the following steps. You must hold the end of the rope in your left hand tightly throughout the process. Pull B in step 4, and align the two

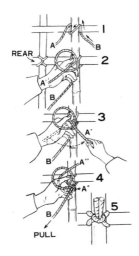

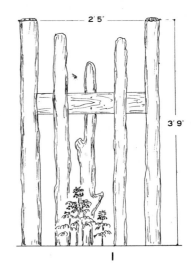

275. *Four-pronged knotting.*

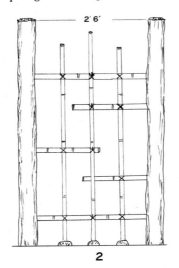

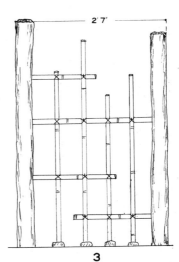

276. *Broken work fences.*

remaining rope ends. Cut them so that about two inches protrude from the knot. These may be nailed or tied together with rope.

Logs with the bark on them cut to different lengths and held in place with a single horizontal brace make a pleasing rustic broken-work fence (Fig. 276-1). Oak or pasania logs with the bark removed and combined with living miscanthus are a pleasing variation on the same fence. Birch logs might blend better with an Occidental house. Planting spear-flower, mandarin orange, fern or pteridophyta at the bottoms of these fences prevents them from seeming too light even though there is no brace at the bottom.

Although the bamboo versions of this fence (Fig. 276-2, 3), which use two log support posts, give the impression of disjointed sections, balance is carefully maintained by running at least one or two horizontal bamboo poles across the entire arrangement.

The rustic and refined teahouse fence in Fig. 277 is made by sinking support posts of chestnut logs with the bark on them, running horizontal braces from side to side, temporarily attaching the bundles of bamboo (*Phyllostachys nigra*) stalks, and finally tying the larger bamboo horizontal retainer pieces in place.

277. Tea-garden fence of bamboo brush.

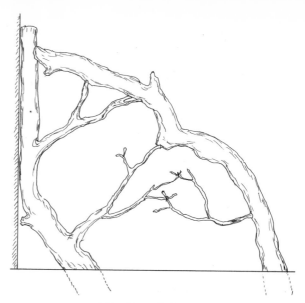

278. Branch fence.

280. Stone-plaque fence.

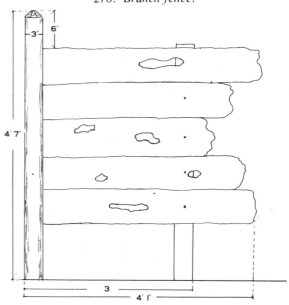

279. Charred board fence.

BRANCH FENCE

Naked branches tied together as shown in Fig. 278 make a very interesting fence when *Clematis florida, Katsura japonica, Trachelospermum asiaticum, Forsythia suspensa,* or morning-glory are planted to entwine through it.

CHARRED BOARD FENCE

After erecting one tall support post and one shorter one, nail boards to them that have interesting holes and that have been charred and scrubbed with a stiff brush to accent the wood grain.

STONE-PLAQUE FENCE

Thin stone plaques bearing poems or other interesting inscriptions can be set as shown in Fig. 280; but they must not be thick or heavy, and they are best partially concealed by plants.

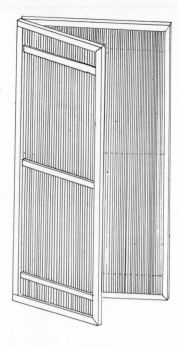

281. Folding-screen fence.

FOLDING-SCREEN FENCE

Useful in shading you from the hot sun or protecting you from the cold breezes, this is more a screen for out of doors than a true fence and should therefore be made of light materials so that it can be moved easily: a frame of one-inch square Japanese cypress or *Magnolia hypoleuca* with a woven reed filler, for instance. Such screens can be made with more than two folds and as tall or as short as circumstances require.

Gates

Instead of absolutely prohibiting passage, fences in Japanese gardens demarcate a limit beyond which it is discourteous to proceed without permission or on the other side of which awaits some new, pleasing experience. This being the case, a simple set of poles and a rope would serve adequately—in fact, the traditional rope used in Shinto shrines, the *shimenawa*, is a case in point. When an element of loveliness is required, however, there are a number of interesting garden gate designs popularly employed. The Saimyoji gate in Fig. 142, though extensively used, is difficult to build unless the maker is familiar with bamboo-working techniques.

Although no definite size can be prescribed for all gates, they are usually as tall or one or two inches shorter than the fence they serve, and about two inches above the ground level. They may be as narrow as two and one-half feet or as wide as four feet, but above this width, ordinary doors are stronger.

TREE-BRANCH GATE

Since lightness is the keynote of these gates, the framework elements should be slender (one inch square, or one inch wide by one and one-quarter inch thick). The gate in Fig. 282, uses two slender horizontals, two intermediate posts of bamboo, and two trimmed branches on one side. Dogwood, *Carpinus lexiflora*, and *Campylaephora hypnaeoides* are good trees to use, but since they rot easily, they should be cut in late autumn or early winter. The two topmost branches are nailed to the upper horizontal to prevent the gate from sagging.

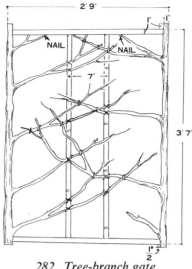

282. Tree-branch gate.

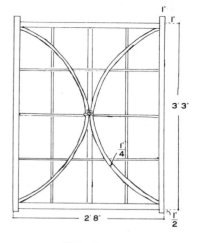

283. Bow gate.

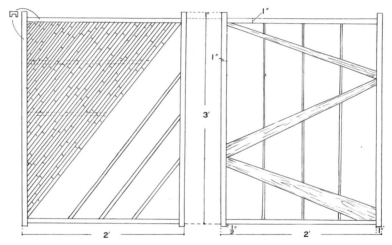

284. Diagonal bamboo and zigzag gates.

Since the branch is likely to split if the nail is driven in carelessly, make a hole with a gimlet first.

BOW GATE (Fig. 283)
Two pieces of split bamboo bent into bows and tied at the middle are inserted in holes prepared in a light frame to make a pleasant, clean gate that is prevented from sagging by the pressure exerted by the two bows.

DIAGONAL BAMBOO GATE (Fig. 284, left)
Unsplit bamboo (one inch thick) inserted diagonally in the upper half of a wooden frame, with only a few diagonals in the lower half, is a striking, fresh gate. The frame should have grooves cut in the verticals and horizontals to hold the bamboo; consequently, the materials should be wider than they are thick. Galvanized wire run through the bamboo will prevent the individual poles from warping. Filling all of the gate as the top half would not only make it heavy, it would also create a commonplace effect.

ZIGZAG GATE

A lightweight frame like the one shown in the right half of Fig. 284 comes to new life when ornamented with a zigzag of boards cut so that increasing widths toward the bottom of the gate add visual stability.

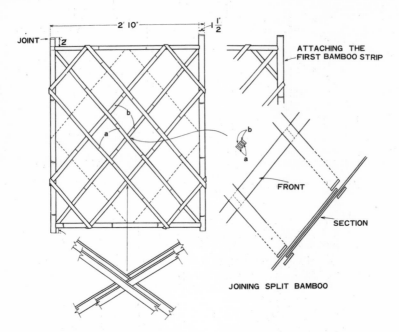

285. Saimyoji gate.

Index

NOTE: Numbers in italics indicate pages
on which illustrations appear.

A
alleyway, 28, *28*

B
bamboo-blind fence, 163
bamboo-brush fence, *166*
bamboo curtain, 164
bamboo gate, 81
  diagonal, 169
bamboo-lattice fence, 163
bamboo-tile fence, 159
bamboo with wide braces, 161
bridge, 157. *See also* stone bridge.
  earth, *63*, 158
  with handrail, 157
  zigzag, 158

C
cha-niwa, 18
chiri ana, 19, 23, *23*
concrete, 144. *See also* garden.
  garden on, 93
  plan of a garden on, *102, 103, 105, 108*

E
entrance, 84

F
fence, 159–162
  bamboo, 159, 163, *166*
  broken-work, 164
  charred-board, 167
  folding-screen, 168
  harp, 164
  stone-plaque, 107
  two-brace open, 162
  unsplit-bamboo, 161
  weir, 161

flume, 20, *46, 75, 100, 109*, 155
fountain, 29
front garden, 28, *37, 47, 53, 75*, 82–86
  with parking space, 83, 84

G
gakumino-ishi, 25, 27
garden
  alleyway, 28, *28*
  beside a parking lot, 111, *111*
  by the beach, 113, *113*

close to house, 89–92
courtyard, 97–99, *97*
  plan of a, *98*
for deserts, 112
for highlands, 111, 112
for hot climate, 112
for seaside regions, 112
for the back of house, 87, 88
for the north, 111, 112
in front of a semi-basement, 91, 92, *91*
in grove, 53–61, *53–55, 59 112*
  plan of a, *56*
indoor, 101–110
inner, *76*
layout of, 114, 115
lawn, 34–52
  plan of a, *35, 37, 42, 45*
  spacious, *35, 36, 39–41, 44–46, 49–51*
on top of concrete, 92–97. *See also* concrete.
rear, *87*
  plan of a, *87*
sand, 31
with a flume, 100
with a ritual water basin, 92
with gravel, 31, *31, 32*, 67, 68, 71, 72
with pond, 61. *See also* pond.
with pond and spring, *29, 30*
with rocks. *See* rock garden.
with shrubbery, *52*
with stone. *See* stone garden.
with tall tree, 29
gate, 168–170
  bow, 169
  tree-branch, 168
  zigzag, 170
gravels, *59. See also* garden.
  patterns in raked, 158, 159
  raked, 68, *72, 73, 91*
  raking, 158
  setting, *58*, 158
  setting raked, 159
  sizes of, 159

H
haiku, 14
hanto, 18, 25

J
japan, subtlety in, 13

K
kabuki, 13
kafuku setchin, 25
kaiseki, 18, 25
kazari setchin, 25
kininguchi, 25
kongokai, 147
kōsen, 20
kyaku, 18

L
lawn hillock, *47*
level masonry, 136

M
mae ishi, 20
mizuya, 22
mortar, compounding ratio of raw materials for, 137, 141, 143

N
nejime, 23
  planting of, 122
nemawashi, 117, 118
nijiriagari fumidanishi, 24
nijiriguchi, 24
Noh, 13, 14

O
onjaku, 18
ori-tsukubai, 20
otsume, 24

P
palisade
  Korean, 162
  open, 162
paper planning, 114
partition fence, *67*
  section, 163–168
paths, construction of, 156
paving stones, 23, *50*, *73*, *92*, 103, 140–143
  arranging, 141
  kinds of, 140, 141
  planning, 141, 142
  setting, 141, 142
planting, 115–123
  root handling, 120–122
  watering, 121, 122
pond, 29, *43*, *50*, *54*, *55*, *59*, *61–64*, *66*, *75*, 144–146, *146*.
  constructing, 144
  drainage, 145
  indoor, 101, *101*
  preparing, 144
  trench, 44
props, 122

R
ritual water basin, *22*, *38*, *88*, *92*, *100*, *106*,

109
  accompanying stones, 152
  drainage, 153
  measurements, *22*
  setting, 152
  types of, 152, 154
rock garden, 31, 33, 67–70, 74, 77, 78, 80, 82, 83, 85, 87–99
roji, 14, 18, 20, 22
  garden, *28*
  inner, 18
  mid, 18
  outer, 18
roots
  handling of, 122
  roles of, 115, 116
  tying, 118
  wrapping, 118, 119
root hairs, roles of, 116
rubble work, *48*
rubble-work wall, *58*, *79*, *83*
  gate with, 84

S
sashi-ishi, 25
sekimori ishi, 20
senzai, 13
shibusa, 13, 14, 18
sozu, 155, 156
spring. *See* garden, pond and spring.
staircase, 157
stepping stones, *23*, *39*, *79*, *104*, *107*, 138, 140
  arranging, 138, 140
  definition of, 138, 140
  large, 140
  planning, 138, 140
  setting, 138, 140
stone
  against a tone wall, *85*
  candle, 20
  capping (or peeping), 15, *15*, *16*, 17, 18
  deciding the placement, of, 124, 125
  flat top, *16*, 18
  front, 20
  hot water-backet, 20
  in courtyard garden, *97*, *98*
  in front garden, *86*
  inclining, *15*, *16*
  long rectangular, 22
  lying down, *16*, 17
  motion of, 18
  peeping, *16*, *17*
  placement of staggered, *88*
  round cut, *16*
  standing, 15, *15*, *16*
  symbolism in, 15–18
  with a shelf-like projection, *16*
stone bridge, *38*, *39*, *50*, *62*, 158
stone force, 18

organization of, 18
stone garden, *31, 32, 46, 68–70, 74, 90, 91, 93, 100*
stone gate, *58*
stone group, *17, 69, 70, 72, 73, 78, 79, 82, 89, 94–96, 103, 105, 110, 111*
  arranging
    one stone, 123–126
    several stones, 126–128
  in stream, *131*
  setting, 123, 132, 133, 137
    order, 137
    rules for, 123, 126
    using wrecker with, 133
stone grouping
  opposition and response in, 129
  principle and subordinate in, 128, 129
  proportions of, 129, 130
  pursuer and pursued in, 128, 129
  rhythm in, 130
  symbolization, 14
  visual and spatial construction of, 126–128
  visual balance of, 128
stone lanterns, *38, 39, 41, 43, 51, 66, 75, 76, 107,* 146, 147, *150*
  composition of, 148
  handling, 148, 149
  proper position of, 147
  setting, 146–148
  stone in front of, 149
  types of, 149, 151
  use of, 33, 35
stone masonry wall, *76*
stone pagoda, *68, 83*
  composition of, 148
  setting, 148
stone-plaque fence, 107
stone root, 123
stone step, *24, 48,* 137, 138
stone tower, *67,* 147–149
  care of, 149
  proper position of, 147, 149
  setting, 148
  types of, 151
stone wall
  informal tortoise-shell pattern, 135
  rubble-work retaining, 134
  standing screen, 135, 136
stream, *13, 81,* 142–144
  bed, *57*
  constructing, 142, 143
  planning, 142

suna setchin, 25
symbolism, 14, 15, 18

T
taizokai, 147
tanzaku ishi, 23, 28
tatami ishi, 20
tea ceremony
  object of, 18
  order of, 22–27
  significance of, 18
tea garden, *21, 65*
  for the Swiss Pines Park, 20
  paving in, 20
  place of, 20
  plan of, *21*
  planting for, 19
  ritual water basin in, 19
  stepping stones in, 20
  stone lantern in, 19
  stones in, 19
teahouse, *64*
  flower arrangement in, 19
  for the Swiss Pines Park, 20
  significance of, 18
  stone step in, 138
  toilet of, 25
  trash hole, 19
  veranda of, *24*
teshoku ishi, 20
tobi ishi, 20
tokonoma, 19, 24
transplanting, 120
  times of, 115
tree
  preparing of, 117, 118
  pruning of, 119, 120
  raising, 118
  roots of, 115, 116
tsukubai, measurements, 20
tsukubai chozubachi, 19

W
wabi, 13, 14
waiting pavilion, *26, 27*
wall, natural-style retaining, 84
waterfall, *40, 55, 60, 64, 75–77, 79,* 130, *131*
watering, 122, 123

Y
yakuishi, 22
yuoke ishi, 20

Z
Zen, 13